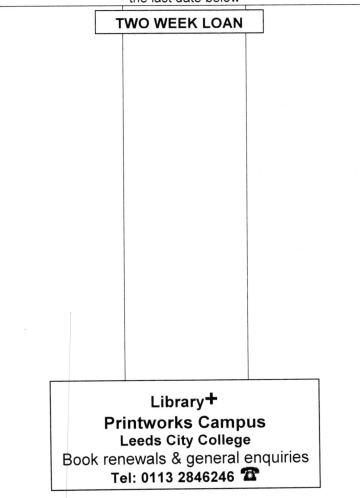

Copyright © 2015 Dr Peter Shaw
Published in 2015 by Marshall Cavendish Business
An imprint of Marshall Cavendish International

1 New Industrial Road, Singapore 536196
genrefsales@sg.marshallcavendish.com
www.marshallcavendish.com/genref

Other Marshall Cavendish Offices:
Marshall Cavendish Corporation. 99 White Plains Road, Tarrytown NY 10591-9001, USA • Marshall Cavendish International (Thailand) Co Ltd. 253 Asoke, 12th Flr, Sukhumvit 21 Road, Klongtoey Nua, Wattana, Bangkok 10110, Thailand • Marshall Cavendish (Malaysia) Sdn Bhd, Times Subang, Lot 46, Subang Hi-Tech Industrial Park, Batu Tiga, 40000 Shah Alam, Selangor Darul Ehsan, Malaysia.

Marshall Cavendish is a trademark of Times Publishing Limited

National Library Board, Singapore Cataloguing-in-Publication Data

Shaw, Peter, Dr, author.
100 great team effectiveness ideas / Dr Peter Shaw.
– Singapore : Marshall Cavendish Business, 2015.
pages cm
ISBN : 978-981-4561-37-2 (paperback)
1. Teams in the workplace – Management. II. Title.
HD66
658.4022 – dc23   OCN899133511

Printed in Singapore by Fabulous Printers Pte Ltd

This book is dedicated to Alan and Kath Briers,

with whom Frances and I have had many great walks and

enjoyable conversations over more than 40 years.

TITLES IN THE 100 **GREAT IDEAS** SERIES

CONTENTS

Section C: Bringing out the best in team members

Section D: Building a new team

Section E: Becoming an even better team leader

Section F: Ensuring effective teams across your organisation

Section G: Being an authoritative team member

Section H: Ensuring effective team development

Section I: Ensuring teams keep learning

Section J: Ensuring continuous learning about leading teams well

ACKNOWLEDGEMENTS

I WANT TO THANK the various leaders who have asked me to work with their teams. It has been a delight to see teams learning together and developing their approach to future opportunities. Those whom I particularly want to thank for giving me the privilege of working with their teams include Suma Chakrabarti, Jonathan Lyle, Caroline Gardner, Sylvo Thijsen, Sarah Davidson, Mel Zuydam, Hazel Mackenzie, Sunil Patel, Shaun McNally, Andrew Scott, Jenni Henderson, Graham Balmer, Kristen McLeod, Helen Stephenson, Katerina Kolyva, Mark Chester, Michael Cross, Pete Lawrence, Kenneth Hogg, Neil Rennick, James Price, John Richardson, Matthew Frost, William Fittall, Stephen Kerr, Antonia Romeo, Jeremy Oates, Jeff Greenman, Diane McGiffen and Mike Foulis. It has been a privilege to see team members reflect on how they bring out the best in each other and raise their sights about what it is possible for a team to deliver.

I am grateful to my supportive colleagues at Praesta Partners, with whom there has been sharing of good practice about working with teams and enabling teams to be the best they can be. Barry Woledge, Paul Gray, Steve Wigzell, Hilary Douglas, Ian Angell and James Thorne have been excellent, supportive colleagues.

Jackie Tookey typed the manuscript with skill and determination, and has always given me constructive feedback on what I am writing. Sonia John-Lewis has managed my diary and time effectively in order to enable me to write. Melvin Neo has been a thoughtful editor who has been a great encourager in my writing books for the '100 Great Ideas' series. Justin Lau has edited the text with great skill and care.

I am very grateful to Sarah Davidson, who has written the foreword to the book. I have known Sarah for a number of years as she has risen to increasingly senior posts in the Scottish Government. Sarah always brings wisdom and clarity of thinking to the way she leads and participates in teams.

I have dedicated this book to Alan and Kath Briers. Alan introduced me to walking in the Yorkshire Dales over 40 years ago. In recent years we have had delightful walks on the Yorkshire Wolds Way, the Alternative Coast to Coast Walk and the Ribble Way, as well as in the French and Austrian Alps.

My family have been very supportive as I have committed time to write this book. Frances and our three children and their spouses regularly tease me about the writing, but always show a reasonably polite interest in the finished product.

I am grateful to you, the reader, for committing your time to dip into the ideas in the book. I hope they are a fruitful source of ideas.

FOREWORD

Whichever sector we work in, whether our contribution is paid or unpaid, whether we operate to a traditional pattern or on a flexible basis, a common denominator for the vast majority of us is the need to collaborate and cooperate in order to get things done. In other words, most of us are members and/or leaders of teams.

Recent years have witnessed a significant shift in our thinking about leadership. Admiration for the so-called 'hero leader' of the past is being replaced by recognition of the human skills necessary to enable people to give of their best – empathy, emotional intelligence, open communication. Increasingly, our performance management systems recognise this by rightly measuring not just *what* we do, but *how* we do it. Feedback from our peers and our staff often contributes to our overall performance assessment. Promotion and recruitment exercises test our ability to motivate, inspire and collaborate with others in order to deliver outcomes. Our understanding of the key drivers of employee engagement points to the importance of high-quality relationships at work.

It is not surprising, therefore, that those aspiring to be good leaders want to know how to lead effective teams.

This is an increasing focus for leadership development just at a time when it is getting ever more challenging to form and direct teams of people who will work together productively and efficiently. Over the past 20 years of my own career, I have witnessed changing dynamics in the workplace leading to more flexible and remote working, the growth of short-term projects with tight delivery schedules, an emphasis on collaborative working across multiple organisations, the concept of the 'virtual team', and the expectation that we will lead and contribute to a number of discrete project teams at any one time. All of these, and other factors, place a high premium on the ability to bring your team to operational maturity as quickly as possible and to support people in working together effectively (and, hopefully, happily) for as long as is required.

My own experience suggests that this won't just 'happen'. Critically, the sum of positive bilateral relationships between the leader and each individual member, while important, will not of itself create an effective team. Similarly, the application of good governance – proportionate programme and project management included – is insufficient on its own to create the conditions for exceptional team performance.

What makes the difference is a thoughtful and sustained dialogue within the team that leads to deeper mutual knowledge and understanding, identifies preferences and capabilities, supports challenge and debate, and allows individual members to build their own influence and contribution to the collective effort. Through this process, expectations of the leader – and the leader's expectations – can also be explored and established in an open forum.

Simply knowing this to be true is, alas, also not sufficient. You and your team need to make a conscious and deliberate investment in each other, and experience suggests that it is useful to have a framework to help initiate and guide the process. I was very fortunate some years ago to be able to draw on Peter Shaw's expertise in offering me exactly that framework through a series of team coaching interventions.

I was struck, and humbled, by the responses of team members to questions posed by Peter such as, 'What brings out the best in you in a team setting?' and 'What was your previous experience of a team that helped you to be confident and effective?' People I thought I knew well in my role as line manager shared personal motivators and experiences that were news to me, let alone to the colleagues with whom they needed to work effectively in order to meet challenging objectives. Explicit bonds of reciprocity were established 'horizontally' across the team in addition to the more traditional 'vertical' management relationships. Team members articulated their 'ask' of me in new ways, reflecting the context of shared endeavour.

None of the questions we worked with in that team coaching process deployed 'rocket science', to use the colloquial expression. Yet, so often, the most obvious approaches are the ones we struggle to find for ourselves. That is the beauty of Peter's approach, encapsulated in this book. Alongside digestible chunks of theory, he offers practical suggestions which bring the ideas to life.

I encourage you to use this book in whatever way is useful to you. It is ideally designed to dip into according to your current circumstances, whether establishing a new team or taking on an existing one, whether in your first role as a team leader or as an experienced leader looking for some refreshment.

Used well, these approaches should help each member of your team to bring the best of themselves and to elicit the best from their colleagues – an excellent basis for whatever it is we are seeking to achieve as leaders, and the experience of work I would wish for everyone.

SARAH DAVIDSON
Director General: Communities
The Scottish Government
Edinburgh, Scotland

INTRODUCTION

THIS BOOK SEEKS to provide prompts to enable teams to thrive and be effective in demanding times.

When a team is working well, productivity is high. Individual competences and differences are recognised. Successes are celebrated and shared. When mistakes happen, they are viewed as times of learning and not failure. But not all teams jell. Frustration can ooze out when there are slight difficulties. The focus can be far too inward-looking and progress slow.

There is a huge interest in how to ensure teams are effective. The pace of change has meant teams have to be quick to adapt. Information technology means that teams have access to much more information, but need to be able to use that information in a constructive and sure-footed way. Globalisation means that there are many more virtual teams which have to find ways of working quickly and effectively, while adapting to cultural differences about expectations and ways of working.

Good team leaders are regularly looking for ways to equip their teams to work effectively at pace, whilst also ensuring there is time to reflect on longer-term issues. There is a growing appetite to keep trying new approaches and learn from the experience of others.

The ideas in this book will provide a range of suggestions to help you calibrate how best you can be both an effective team leader and member. The book is divided into ten sections, looking in turn at:

- Observing teams that work well
- Taking on leading an existing team
- Bringing out the best in team members

- Building a new team

- Becoming an even better team leader

- Ensuring effective teams across your organisation

- Being an authoritative team member

- Ensuring effective team development

- Ensuring teams keep learning

- Ensuring continuous learning about leading teams well

The book is designed so you can dip into the different sections. It can be used by individuals or teams. It is intended to be a practical tool for managers and leaders at any level, in any organisation, in any country.

I have drawn from my first career working in the public sector for 32 years and then a second career working in the private sector for 12 years, alongside a number of roles within the voluntary sector. In addition I have worked with teams across five continents, ranging from international executive boards to local community teams. It has been a privilege to draw from experience in such a wide range of contexts and to see teams deliver outcomes they never thought possible.

I hope the ideas in the book provide valuable prompts for thought and action as you participate in a range of different teams.

OBSERVING TEAMS THAT WORK WELL

WHY DO TEAMS MATTER?

OBSERVING WHEN TEAMS make a difference to overall outcomes, as well as being cognisant of the contribution of individuals, enables you to develop your own understanding of why teams matter.

The idea

When I begin working with a team, I ask team members to reflect on teams they have been part of in the past that have worked well and to identify the characteristics of those teams. I suggest that they think about teams from different spheres – a sports team, a choir, a community organisation, a faith group, a family unit, or a work team in a different organisation that they were part of.

I invite them to share their observations on what binds a good team together and what makes it effective. We then talk about outcomes that the teams delivered and the extent to which operating as a team makes a difference to the prospect of success.

The stories that are shared are often about how members of a team bring different skills and experiences. In good teams, forward thinking is developed in dialogue as individuals build on each other's ideas. The sense of shared endeavour, the working up of ideas together, and the resolve that comes from a common purpose mean that the team becomes 'more than the sum of its parts'.

A telling characteristic of a good team is its ability to provide support to its members and constructive challenge during periods when the team's resilience is being tested. A team with clarity about reality and boldness of intent reinforces the courage of its members and their belief that they are acting responsibly.

When Miranda was appointed as a Director in a Government Department, she began to reflect on what type of senior team she wanted to develop. She had been part of teams in the private sector before, and was a lay member of a leadership team in a church. She had observed at first hand the positive benefits of a team working well together.

When working in a marketing agency, the team was at its best when it was developing a creative idea and building on members' contributions. In a previous role in Government, the teams were most effective when they were interrelating evidence and facts with practical opportunities. In the voluntary sector, the team worked at its best when participants were able to play to their strengths and be honest about the practical constraints on the time they could give.

By drawing from her experience in three very different sectors, Miranda could see the benefits and pitfalls that came from working with diverse and often opinionated team members.

In practice

- Reflect on the range of teams you have been part of and why they were successful

- Note down the generic characteristics of teams you have been part of that worked well

- Seek the views of others on why teams matter and see how much overlap there is with your perspective

- Reflect on what would have happened in particular situations if you had not been part of a team, and to what extent the outcomes would have been less good

2 WHEN CAN A TEAM HELP YOU BE EFFECTIVE?

REFLECTING ON WHEN a team can help you be effective will sharpen your understanding of a good team and your commitment to make a team work well.

The idea

A team can help you be more effective when it has a positive reputation on which you can build. Being a member of a credible team opens doors for you. The input of other members of the team might give you a wider set of perspectives and enable you to develop your own thinking. Constructive challenge from members of the team might enable you to sift ideas into the practicable and not so practicable.

It is worth recalling when fellow team members' contributions and influences shaped your thinking about the art of the possible. Perhaps interaction with a colleague enabled you to have the courage of your convictions to take forward action when you were hesitant. Or perhaps a colleague forewarned you of a problem or correctly anticipated the views of other people.

Being part of a team can help you be more effective through a combination of discussions in team meetings, planned meetings with other team members, informal conversations, and steers in writing between meetings. A good team dynamic helps outside the meeting room too. You can be carrying in your head the wisdom of your colleagues as you reflect on their perspectives and insights on different issues. Perhaps a colleague's advice to 'do what you think is right' can be a mantra that helps you reach a point of decision after weighing up the evidence.

Miranda was always grateful to the members of her team in the marketing organisation, who encouraged her to develop her ideas and turn them into practical propositions. The team encouraged her to stretch her thinking and forced her to test out how robust her ideas were. Miranda knew she had the support of her colleagues, and recognised that the team's effectiveness flowed from this robust awareness of each other's ideas.

Miranda recognised that she would be given a hard time when her ideas were examined from different perspectives. She also knew that at the end of what felt like an interrogation, there would be moments of laughter and what felt like a 'virtual hug' as people left the room feeling it had been a constructive meeting with ideas turning into next steps. The debate could feel painful, but the team had developed an honest, rigorous approach that worked well within a supportive environment.

In practice

- Reflect on teams you have been part of that helped develop you as an effective team member

- What was the contribution of others in such teams that enabled you to grow in confidence and effectiveness?

- How much of the benefit for you of being part of a team resulted from the knowledge of your colleagues, or their ability to help you develop your ideas and have the courage of your convictions?

- Which team had the biggest positive effect on you and why?

3 WHEN IS A TEAM NOT A TEAM?

A TEAM MAY LOOK to be working effectively, but probing where a team is not maximising its potential can provide revealing insights for any new team leader or member.

The idea

Members of a team may look as if they are engaging and listening to each other in a team meeting or a team event. But as soon as they move out of the company of their colleagues, they operate as individuals rather than as part of a coherent team.

Members of a team might not be acting as a team partly because of the absence of any comments of support from team colleagues. There may be no words of criticism, but the absence of explicit words of support may give the impression that the team is not that important.

It can be helpful to imagine yourself as an observer of the teams you are part of. When do you see such a team in dialogue, building each other up, supporting each other and challenging each other in a way that is constructive and leads to better outcomes? In some teams, you may notice that what is said in a team meeting is not fully lived out in conversations and actions between meetings. As you observe the body language that team members display to each other, it can often be painfully clear where there is respect and a keenness to engage, and where there is scepticism and mistrust.

Miranda felt ambivalent about the leadership team she was part of in her church. She recognised that her contribution to this team could only be limited because she had a full-time job. Miranda was fully committed in the meetings she was present at but felt undercurrents as different team members had different priorities, with an inner circle of people who were able to commit more time than she could.

Miranda debated in her own mind whether it was inevitable that such a team would not be entirely at ease with itself. Miranda suggested that the leadership team spent a Saturday morning reflecting on the extent to which the team was working effectively. There was some progress in the resulting conversation, but there were clearly underlying assumptions that were deeply felt about appropriate levels of commitment. This meant that the team was unlikely to be as open and creative as Miranda had hoped.

In practice

- Bring your own perspective about when a team is working well and when it could be a lot better

- Observe how much of a team dynamic continues purposefully between meetings

- Observe how team agreements can be undermined by the words and behaviours of participants between team events

- Reflect on how a greater degree of openness and honesty can be encouraged, so participants are conscious of where they are not operating well as a team

- Be realistic about the limitations on how much more effective a team can be because of the personalities or circumstances

4 WHAT CHARACTERISES TEAMS THAT ADAPT WELL TO CHANGING CIRCUMSTANCES?

Understanding which teams adapt well to changing circumstances gives a clear insight into the characteristics of teams that are likely to continue to be effective.

The idea

The way a team adapts to changing circumstances is both about tasks and mutual obligations, and about attitudes and support. A good team ensures that the individual who is leading in the handling of an unexpected event receives both practical and emotional support from colleagues.

Some changes in circumstances are permanent rather than the result of short-term crises or pressures. A new chief executive is appointed with a different set of objectives and a different way of doing business. The context has radically changed. There is no going back. A team that adapts well is not hankering after the previous chief executive. It accepts the inevitability of a new chief executive and sees the opportunities. There may be a sense of passing grief or disappointment but the team has to move into a constructive and positive space quickly, without forgetting all the learning of past months.

An adaptive team uses its shared history as a means of bonding together and not constraining its future, combining realism about changing circumstances with a recognition of its track record of capability and delivery. There will be core values about how the team works together that enable the team to adapt to changing circumstances. Adaptability becomes a key strength provided there is a good level of self-assessment by the team about why and how it is adapting.

Miranda observed how her previous team had responded to having a new Government Minister. They recognised that they needed to grieve for a short period about the loss of the relationship with the previous, highly respected minister. At the same time, they knew they had to move on quickly to serve the new minister without hesitation or deviation.

Emotionally the journey took a few weeks, but practically they adapted their approach and way of working within a few days. What helped was the presence in the team of a couple of people who had worked for a number of different Government Ministers and who were well attuned to making a speedy adjustment so that the new minister experienced loyal civil servants who understood what was important to her.

In practice

- Observe how different teams respond to changing circumstances and adapt their roles and expectations

- Reflect on how the teams you have been part of recognised changing circumstances and responded to them in a constructive way

- How did the teams you have been part of use past experience to good effect?

- What are the key characteristics, from your observations, of teams that adapt well to changing circumstances?

5 WHAT HAVE YOU LEARNT FROM CONTRIBUTING TO A TEAM THAT WORKED WELL?

IT IS ALWAYS WORTH asking yourself what has been your contribution to teams that you have been part of that worked well, and then building those strengths and approaches into your way of leading future teams.

The idea

I often ask team members to reflect on the learning about their contribution to successful teams. I deliberately ask them to draw learning from their participation in teams in different sectors. A value of encouraging this reflection is to highlight the development of their contribution over time and recognise how their repertoire of approaches has widened.

Sometimes, people recall past ways of contributing that have since become less influential. The memory of being part of a successful team at university can rekindle a belief that the individual could contribute in a more liberated or creative way. Sometimes the constraints of working in a bureaucracy may have dampened the individual's confidence in their ability to be a catalyst in a team.

Valuable parallels can also be drawn from being part of a family. Parents develop a much wider range of influencing skills because of the need to manage the lives of their children and the family unit. A family with young children has to be supportive and clear about rules of engagement. There are often eureka moments in my coaching conversations when individuals recognise that skills they have developed in leading and influencing within the family are readily transferable into the work environment.

Miranda was part of a group that walked in Scotland each May. The responsibility for organising the walk rotated over the years. There was a shared commitment to make the walks enjoyable and challenging. There was trust in those who planned the walks and a lot of encouragement and laughter.

The learning for Miranda from being part of this team was about the passing on of leadership responsibility, the willingness of each individual to contribute to the success of the overall venture and the encouragement and support if individuals were finding a particular climb tough. They delighted in doing an activity together which they all enjoyed. There was a mix of engaging in each other's company in silence and lively conversations. Miranda sought to build into her team activities this blend of quiet reflection and active discussion.

In practice

- Keep crystallising your learning from your contribution in different teams

- Recall the type of contribution you made to teams in your early twenties and reflect on whether you have lost some of the sparkle you showed then

- Be mindful of how your repertoire of contributions has varied in different teams and how you have responded to different members of a team

- Be alert to the transferable learning from being part of a family or part of a social activity

- Focus your next steps on building on what has worked well rather than being absorbed with what has worked less well

WHEN HAVE YOU HELPED TURN A TEAM AROUND?

RECALLING WHEN YOU HELPED turn a team around reinforces your understanding of your own capability to see reality and to influence others well.

The idea

As you recall being a member of different teams, you bring back to your mind situations where you were influential. Perhaps you made a comment that made people stop and think whether the direction of travel was right. Or perhaps you asked a question that set off a conversation that led to an unexpected conclusion.

There may have been occasions when you were able to put your mark on a team quickly. If a team is stuck and recognises that it needs fresh ideas, a new member will be welcomed with open arms and become influential quickly.

On other occasions, the team you joined may have been very established in the way it worked. As a new person, you might have thought your voice was not going to be influential. However, by virtue of an individual's demeanour and questions, they can have an impact right from the start if they bring an alertness to changing circumstances and the ability to listen well and play back what they observe. A new member can turn around the tone of a team quickly through bringing a sense of curiosity, a lightness of touch and the ability to interrelate reality and opportunity. Over time, you will build up experience, credibility and influence.

Miranda recalled a team she had joined in the marketing organisation where, initially, she had not felt welcomed. By being persistent in her questions and always listening to what other members were saying, she gradually became accepted as a valued member of the team.

Miranda brought a realism about how a particular market worked and what would be crucial to success in bringing a new product into that market. Her learning from this experience was the importance of believing that you have a worthwhile contribution to make and being dogged in focusing on what you think is most important, alongside bringing an engaging and collaborative approach.

In practice

- Be clear in your own mind what needs to change
- Highlight the problems without being critical of team members
- Be deliberate in the use of questions to bring home harsh reality
- Take pride in when you have been able to influence a team and turn it around
- Identify what you did to help turn a team around and embed that approach firmly in your repertoire of approaches
- Seek feedback from others about how your actions contributed to turning a team around

WHAT HAVE BEEN THE INGREDIENTS OF THE SHARED PURPOSE OF A SUCCESSFUL TEAM?

HAVING A SHARED PURPOSE is integral to the success of a team. The shared purpose may be at a number of different levels.

The idea

A sports team has the shared purpose of winning a game or a competition. A project team has the shared purpose of delivering a successful project on time and within budget. A construction team has the shared purpose of erecting a sound building that will not fall down. The overall, overt, shared purpose will be underpinned by the purposes of different groups of specialists, as well as shared understandings about how the organisation and teams are going to work together.

There should, for all teams, be a shared purpose about the overall outcome, but shared purposes might also be about the effectiveness of collaboration between different groups and the development of skills and ways of working. An integrated team will have a shared purpose for the overall team, as well as purposes that sub-groups or pairs of members share.

There may be cross-cutting remits that are best taken forward by a couple of team members rather than individuals. Perhaps someone with operational experience might be paired with someone more experienced in policy development in order to think through how best to improve communication within an organisation. It can have long-term benefits to identify team members who do not naturally link with each other and give them a remit to develop thinking about next steps in a cross-cutting area in which they both have some interest.

In Miranda's experience, the teams that worked particularly well often also had a shared purpose of developing staff effectiveness and building better relationships with stakeholders, or improving the effectiveness and adaptability of certain parts of the organisation. This suggested that a team that worked well had interlinking shared purposes, some of which were quantifiable and some of which were less tangible. Her perspective was that you needed a combination of numerical outcome targets alongside purposes that were more geared to emotional understanding and personal growth in confidence and effectiveness.

In practice

- Reflect on what have been the links between shared purpose and a team being successful

- Reflect on the extent to which there is a shared purpose in the teams you are currently a member of

- How have you built a shared purpose for teams you led in the past?

- To what extent do you think that a shared purpose needs numerical and emotional levels?

- To what extent is it helpful to build a network of interlocking shared purposes involving team members in different combinations?

8 WHAT HAS BEEN AN EFFECTIVE RELATIONSHIP BETWEEN RATIONAL AND EMOTIONAL CONSIDERATIONS?

INTERLINKING THE RATIONAL and emotional in the way teams operate and are led is crucial to success.

The idea

The rational and emotional parts of our brains process information at different speeds. The emotional reactions tend to kick in first, with rational reactions needing time to catch up.

An effective team will have emotional rapport as well as the ability to have rational debate. Good-quality emotional rapport is not just about people liking each other, though that helps. It is about a strength of trust and respect which flows from an underlying closeness and warmth, together with the freedom for people to challenge assumptions and express strongly felt differences.

When a selection panel is appointing a new member to a team, the rational debate is about someone's experience and how it matches the competences. Reaching the right answer at the rational level is a necessary – but not fully sufficient – part of the process. Whatever the words used when members select a new team member, they are reflecting on the degree of rapport and whether they would like to work with the potential candidate. The question, 'Do I want this person in my team?' is inevitably both about technical competences and the belief that there will be enough emotional rapport for the dialogue to work effectively and lead to constructive outcomes.

If there is emotional friction between members of a team, the ability to have rational dialogue is much diminished. The good team leader thinks through how to ensure good-quality, realistic and rigorous debate, and how to build up rapport, mutual respect and emotional support across the whole team.

Miranda was conscious that in the church leadership team, the emotional considerations could be detrimental to rational discussion. She respected the passion and energy that some of the team members brought, but was aware that their perspectives could sometimes be blinkered and not take account of the pressures of the working world or some of the wider debates in society.

Miranda's main contribution to the team was to recognise the emotional considerations that were important to her colleagues and then bring the discussion back to the choices that needed to be made and the factors that needed to be considered. Miranda brought a level-headed approach that tried to link together the passion to make a difference with the reality of financial constraints. She was careful not to dampen enthusiasm unnecessarily: her aim was to steer it and not destroy it.

In practice

- Recognise in yourself the different speeds at which your rational and emotional reactions kick in

- Understand how teams operate at both the rational and emotional levels

- See how rational and emotional considerations can best be combined

- Encourage teams to do self-reflection about how they operate at the rational and emotional levels, and how the two levels interlink

9 HOW HAVE GOOD TEAMS USED DIFFERENCE TO GOOD EFFECT?

MAKING GOOD USE OF DIVERSITY – in expertise, age, culture and gender, among other areas – is the mark of all successful teams.

The idea

An obvious source of diversity is the type of professional background or experience that individual members bring. A team running an organisation, irrespective of its size, needs people with expertise in finance, operations, human relations and policy development. Valuable differences flow from the nature of people's experiences in different sectors or organisations of different sizes.

Valuable differences can also come through different cultural and religious perspectives, family circumstances, geographic and cultural backgrounds, and differences of age and gender. The more global teams become, the more important is respect for cultural differences and the capacity to recognise what will bring out the best in people and the type of behaviours that are appropriate.

One team I was part of was highly capable and effective in many ways, but there was a white male preoccupation with football. Other teams I have known have banned talking about subjects that tend to appeal to only one dominant sub-group. Respect for difference has to be worked at so that those members of a team who feel in a minority are drawn into full participation in the team and not left isolated.

The teams that are most effective at handling the balance between the short-term and the long-term often have a good gender balance. Such teams tend not to rush into poorly thought through conclusions made in the heat of the moment. The question for any leader is how best to create a good balance of different perspectives within a team in a way that stimulates creativity and draws in a wider perspective, while not inhibiting the team from reaching conclusions.

Miranda observed how her previous boss, John, had used difference to good effect. John always ensured that the perspectives of different people were heard. He ensured people with different temperaments, specialisms and ages worked on projects together.

If John spotted the men going into a huddle, he broke it up promptly. He was directive in asking people to work in small groups, bringing together those with very different experiences. Miranda observed how John did this mixing up systematically, always giving clear explanations for what he was doing.

In practice

- See diversity in a team as a strength and not a liability
- Build as much diversity into a team as possible
- Mix together people of different specialisms, genders, ages and cultures so that issues are dealt with in a way that recognises that there will always be different perspectives to take into account
- Talk about what is distinctive in you, and respect and recognise what is distinctive in others
- Draw attention to the progress that is made when people use difference to good effect

WHAT HAS ENABLED EFFECTIVE TEAMS TO COPE WELL IN A CRISIS?

OBSERVING WHAT ENABLES TEAMS to be effective in a crisis reveals something about their depth of relationship and resilience.

The idea

A team may often not realise how strong it is or how fragile it has become until it goes through a crisis. A team that does well in tough times is able to draw on the relationships and reserves it has built up over a period. Once a team has been through one crisis, it learns new ways of working that will equip it for future challenges. A team that cracks early in a crisis, on the other hand, probably needs to be 'deconstructed' and a new team formed.

Teams need to maintain core attitudes and beliefs no matter how much pressure they come under, tackling each challenge clearly and calmly, and leading from the front to inspire those around them. Team members must look after themselves in order to maintain stamina and well-being for an exhausting period.

The good team in turbulent times will be able to be honest about what is going wrong and will be able to recognise when it is about to lose it. It will have the capacity to focus its energy and time. There will be those in the team who are able to bring a positive mindset, no matter how intractable the challenge may be. A good team leader in a crisis focuses on what can be done rather than what has gone wrong.

A key test for any team in turbulent times is to keep a sense of perspective. Teams that do this well are getting the best data and information they can; they listen to the views of those who are observing what the team is doing, and they create space, however brief, for reflection. An experienced mentor or advisor may serve as a sounding board, enabling the team to keep a reasonably balanced perspective about what is going on.

Miranda drew positive lessons from the part she played in a team in a marketing organisation when it faced financial crisis. She observed a team leader, Jean, who was level-headed and focused. Jean brought clarity about issues and an ability to focus conversations on what was possible going forward rather than being too preoccupied with how the problems had occurred. Problems were rigorously examined and options worked through in a dignified and unemotional way. Miranda observed Jean both pushing team members hard and being concerned about their well-being. Jean ensured there was humour and there was down-time, with the opportunity for team members to reflect and become refreshed.

In practice

- Be clinical in recognising how leaders have led teams well in crises

- Observe what enables a team to be focused on addressing problems and open to new information at the same time

- Remember what kept you resilient in turbulent times and think through how you could enable others to keep up their resilience in demanding situations

- Be prepared to lead your team through a crisis by balancing both focused activity and space for renewal and refreshment

- Reflect on what are the underlying shared values that enable teams to cope well in turbulent times

TAKING ON LEADING AN EXISTING TEAM

11. UNDERSTAND ITS HISTORY AND THE EMOTIONS

UNDERSTANDING THE HISTORY and the emotions of a team is crucial to appreciating how the team will react in a new situation.

The idea

Every team has its successes and failures – which may or may not be talked about. Participants may be shy or hesitant to talk about successes as they may not want to look as if they are dwelling on the past. But when a team or team members are encouraged to talk about previous successes, it draws out the strengths of the team and the confidence they have in their own track record.

Equally, a team may have been bruised by past experiences. There may be feelings of inadequacy about having been caught off-guard, and a lack of confidence to tackle new situations boldly.

Understanding emotions is just as important as understanding facts. When a team is invited to talk about its history, are the visible emotions pleasure and laughter, or unease and hesitation? Do team members look up with a smile or look down with a frown? Asking a team what have been the dominant emotions in their meetings over recent months can be revealing. If the emotions expressed are frustration or helplessness, there is much to explore using these key words to open up the effects of recent history.

When Jeff took on the leadership of an IT project, he had an open session with the team. He asked them to talk through what they were most proud of and what they felt were the strengths of the team. He then played back to them themes he picked up from these stories, which had been told with energy and clarity. Next,

Jeff asked the team to talk through what had gone less well and what their learning had been. As they described different events, he asked about their emotions, which ranged from disappointment with themselves to resentment about a rapidly changing agenda.

The description of their emotions provided Jeff with clear insights into what the team had been feeling and how it might be approaching the future. Jeff went on to ask the team members what pointers they drew from their emotional journey that would be relevant to the way they wanted him to lead the team going forward.

In practice

- Invite a team to talk about key events in its history

- Create a context where a team can reflect dispassionately on what it has learnt from its own history

- Invite a team to describe its dominant emotions over recent months and the evolution of those emotions

- Use conversations with individual team members to cross-check what you are hearing from the team as a whole

- Follow the emotions that are described in a reflective way through asking questions in order to fully understand what has been happening

- Look out for emotional bruises that are still there and be mindful how you handle them

12 UNDERSTAND THE CHARACTERS, MOTIVATIONS AND EXPECTATIONS

SEEKING TO UNDERSTAND team members' characters, motivations and expectations quickly helps you use their skills and energy to best effect without a long introductory period.

The idea

A valuable approach when taking on a new team is to be curious about what makes team members tick. There is a risk that early conversations are all about tasks. A better way to begin a relationship is to ask individual team members what their motivations are. An open question such as 'What do you most enjoy about your job?' will elicit insights about an individual's work and personality. Follow-up questions like 'What in your job motivates you most, and what motivates you least?' then help you paint a fuller picture of the personality you are working with.

Questions about expectations might cover 'What are your expectations about what the team should deliver going forward?' It can also be helpful to ask team members about their personal expectations of what they want you to deliver in your role.

The assessments you are beginning to make are about the character of the individuals who make up the team and how those characters interact with each other. You are developing a picture about their strengths and their foibles. You are building an understanding about their levels of resilience and how they maintain their resolve when the going gets tough. You will probably have received a briefing from your predecessor and others in the organisation, but it is crucial to reach your own conclusions, taking account of the view of others while not being overwhelmed by views that are partial or outdated.

Jeff spent time with each of his team members asking about their motivations and expectations for the future. He asked open questions and ensured that he followed up on any emotions that were described. He played back to each team member in summary form what he was hearing from them so that they recognised that their new boss understood them.

Jeff took delight in learning about the character and journey of each of his team members. He built an understanding about the topics that it would be good to raise with them from time to time so that he was in touch with their evolving motivations and expectations.

In practice

- Be open in asking what motivates team members

- Give quality time to let team members talk about their motivations and expectations

- Build a picture in your mind of the personality of each team member, their values and degree of resilience

- Identify points that you can come back to in order to keep alert to their evolving motivations and expectations

- Treat others' views on your team members seriously but come to your own conclusions

- Delight in the differences in the characteristics of your team members

13 UNDERSTAND WHERE SPONSORS ARE COMING FROM

KEEPING AN UP-TO-DATE PERSPECTIVE of where sponsors are coming from is essential to providing a framework within which to decide where to focus the skills and energy of the team.

The idea

The key sponsors may not always be obvious. For most teams there will be an individual or committee to whom they are accountable. Being clear about the accountability line is important for shaping the work of a team or group. The key people may be two or three members of a committee, or there may be individuals or groups who are providing funds who have more influence than might immediately be apparent. Or there may be an influential figure in the background whose views are sought by team members.

A key question to ask when taking on an existing team might be, 'Whose views carry the most weight when it comes to measuring our success?' Some sponsors will be obvious and fully committed to the work of the team. Other sponsors may be watching with interest and only be willing to give wholehearted support when they see a team beginning to make serious progress.

Another question worth asking is, 'Which sponsors are likely to be sceptical?' These are the ones you'll need to invest the most time in. It is worth scoring your sponsors out of ten on their commitment to your team's objectives. This simple device will give you a clear perspective of where to invest your time.

Jeff was fairly clear what his boss wanted his team to deliver; he was more concerned about some of the other senior figures in the organisation, who he sensed were more sceptical about the team's abilities. He sought intelligence through his own networks about which individuals had expressed scepticism about his new team, then ensured that he had one-to-one conversations with each of them to understand more about their reservations.

Jeff also constructed a map in his mind of the influential people in the organisation who could become sponsors for what his team were trying to deliver. With each of these individuals, he tried to find points of mutual interest in order to build a sense of common purpose going forward. In this way he was building a network of informal sponsors.

In practice

- Be clear who your formal sponsors are and invest time and energy in those relationships

- Have a timetable for keeping in touch with key sponsors so you are aware if their views change

- Beware of an over-reliance on two or three sponsors

- Recognise who are the influential people who will have views on the work of your team and build a relationship with them

- Build new sponsors for your team where there can be a win-win outcome

- Keep close to the gossip network to understand what influential people are saying about your team

14 UNDERSTAND HOW COMMUNICATION HAPPENS

I⊤ IS IMPORTANT ⊤O understand both the formal and informal communication arrangements between team members, as well as between the team and the wider organisation, and then to work with the grain of these arrangements.

The idea

Every team has formal and informal means of communication. While there may be official team meetings with minutes describing their conclusions, communication also takes place in more subtle ways. It is about building alliances and shared agendas, and incorporates an underlying awareness of how priorities are changing and where the power balance lies between different interests.

Communication in a team is critically about what happens outside of formal meetings. Do members of the team meet informally over lunch or in the pub? What is the pattern of bilaterals and trilaterals that occur? How much of the communication is spoken or unspoken? Have members of the team been working together over a long period, and as a consequence are they able to read each other's thoughts using a few coded phrases?

Asking the question, 'How does communication happen in this team?' is not likely to give you a full answer. So much communication is done without pre-planning. Team members often find it difficult to describe the nature of the communication that happens quite spontaneously within the team.

What is important is to watch how communication happens. It can be helpful to seek the views of both team members and those who observe the team in action. When you take over a team, you want to build an understanding about how positive messages gain credibility in the team, and when negative thoughts lead to a downward spiral that saps resolve and energy.

Jeff recognised that there were two particularly influential people in his team. If these two individuals were speaking with a similar voice to his, then a unified message could be communicated across the whole team. He invested in these two people because he saw them as key opinion formers. Jeff understood that informal communication was important, but recognised there needed to be more rigour about the formal communication between team members about priorities and the sharing of intelligence and expertise. He was determined to model the type of open communication that would be important for the on-going effectiveness of the team.

In practice

- Build a clear picture of the pattern of communication within the team

- Identify who the key opinion formers are and how they communicate with others

- Accept the importance of a combination of formal and informal communication in any team

- Be mindful what type of communication raises motivation and energy, and what type saps these attributes

- Think through where you intervene best in order to influence in a positive way the type of communication that is happening within your team and with those outside the team

15   LISTEN IN ORDER TO UNDERSTAND

WHEN TAKING ON AN existing team, the first step is listening in order to understand; it is not about setting a direction and taking control.

The idea

As a new leader of a team, you will find that those who appointed you will want to see you take control and ensure the work is taken forward. The drive for progress and delivery may seem overriding.

But the first step is to listen and not to rush into irreversible action. Listening well has potentially profound consequences. Asking key questions and then listening intently will require your team members to articulate their narratives well. If there are inconsistencies in the way the team works, they may well recognise these in the process of telling their narratives.

Getting team members, customers, other colleagues, and staff to tell of their experiences and their expectations will give you excellent data about whether there is alignment or not.

Prompts like 'Tell me more about the progress you have made, or about some of the frustrations on the way' can give insights about what you, as the new team leader, can unblock or promote. Having listened to a wide range of different views, there will almost inevitably be an underlying pattern with key themes that need to be addressed.

The best way of getting commitment from team members is to demonstrate you have listened to them by playing back a summary of the themes you heard. The summary enables you to bring together the perspectives of different people and to describe overriding impressions in a graphic way. You may think that this analysis should lead to you describing the necessary action; however, it is often good to hold back to see whether the team members, having heard the themes you are playing back, volunteer to take action themselves.

Jeff recognised that the team had become complacent and needed to sharpen their priorities going forward, but he decided not to say that explicitly. Having listened to a range of different people, he played back to the team some of the themes he was hearing about a lack of sharpness and responsiveness.

In a thoughtful conversation as a team, some of the key members talked about the need for a greater sense of priority going forward. Jeff built upon their comments by asking further questions. The end result was a much clearer set of priorities without Jeff having to impose them.

In practice

- Always invest in listening rather than telling in the early stages

- Ask open-ended questions

- Ask the same questions to people inside the team and outside it

- Keep summarising what you are hearing and play back generic themes

- Be clear in your own mind what action might be needed, but try to frame conversations so that others in the team come up with the action

PACE YOUR INTERVENTIONS

IT IS IMPORTANT TO differentiate between when you need to act quickly and when wider discussion is needed before decisions are made.

The idea

When you take over leading an existing team, there can be a personal desire to make an early impact. There may also be pressing decisions that need to be made. Things might have festered during an interregnum, or the previous leader might have deliberately left decisions for the incoming leader to handle. Sometimes part of the brief when starting a new job is that early decisions need to be taken. Often the advice to a new leader is to secure some 'early wins'.

However, a wrong decision is worse than a delayed decision. It is important that decisions are not made just for the sake of making decisions. Any early decisions need to be articulated clearly so people understand your reasoning and how you have taken into consideration what you have heard since arriving in the role.

It is helpful to recognise with your team that a decision needs to be taken on a particular timescale, with members having clear opportunities to contribute to discussion before the final decision is made. A decision taken within a month of arriving in a new role may seem rushed, but if you had identified in the first week that a decision needed to be made within a month for particular reasons, the potential criticism of acting in haste is much diminished.

As you listen to debate within the team, you will want to be mindful about how you pace your interventions. If there are values or perspectives which you think are critical, it can be worth making these points early. With an established team, however, you will probably want to listen to the debate for quite a time before you intervene in a way that steers conclusions.

Jeff knew that certain issues needed to be sorted quickly. There needed to be more honesty within the team about progress on different projects. Jeff insisted on clear, open reporting right from the start.

Jeff had some concerns about the balance of skills within the team. He raised questions with different parties and distilled the feedback, so that when a couple of vacancies arose in the team, he had clarity about the type of people he wanted to appoint.

Jeff was clear about the values of openness, transparency and boldness. He kept reinforcing these behaviours in members of the team by praising them when their actions were consistent with these values. Jeff was willing to be repetitive in talking about the behaviours that were important, but was selective about how he intervened when different projects were discussed, limiting his interventions to key strategic points.

In practice

- Accept that if you intervene too much, you will sap motivation and risk being ignored

- Be willing to intervene using questions rather than statements

- Deliberately vary the pace at which you intervene depending on the importance of the subject and your judgement about how well the issue is being handled

- If there is silence, do not feel you have to intervene with a conclusion

17 BE CLEAR ON THE DIRECTION

WHEN TAKING OVER LEADERSHIP of a team, there is a need to be clear on the direction of travel, which should be expressed simply and unequivocally.

The idea

Being clear about the direction is rarely about a short, bold statement that bears no relationship to what happened before. When you take over leading an existing team, there will be questions about the effect of your arrival. Sometimes what matters is a reiteration of the purpose of the team – 'Our task continues to be to deliver this key project, or reform, or set of outcomes'. An unequivocal re-affirmation of the intent of a team solidifies the framework within which existing work can continue.

Sometimes you will have been appointed to lead a team because there are new, externally imposed goals. Part of your initial impact as team leader follows from the clarity and confidence with which you describe those goals and your narrative about why those goals are reasonable and doable.

On other occasions, you may be called on early to review a policy or a process to decide whether or not it is appropriate. Your clarity might be about the timescale and terms of the review, so that there is an effective staging of decisions.

Jeff knew that it was important to his new team that he set a clear direction about the quality of work they did and the nature of their relationship with customers. He was convinced that the working relationship with key customers needed to improve. He was clear about this intent and set in process a review of existing customer relationships on a defined timescale. He kept up the momentum through engaging personally with key customers and ensuring that their concerns were followed up on.

There were certain areas where Jeff knew he had to be insistent and repetitive about the direction of travel, so that team members recognised the importance of what the overall team delivered rather than merely fulfilling personal agendas.

In practice

- Recognise the direction of travel you inherit and be clear in your own mind how much of that is a given, how much you believe is right, and how much it is realistic to seek to change

- Be clear in your messages on the direction of travel and ensure they are unequivocal and repeated often

- Ensure that the rationale and evidence for your clarity of direction are clearly communicated

- Keep listening to trusted people to get feedback on whether your sense of direction is valid and coherent

- Stand back and observe your own rhetoric to check that it is believable

18 MAINTAIN MOMENTUM AS TEAM MEMBERS CHANGE

THE ARRIVAL OF NEW MEMBERS to a team provides an opportunity to affirm the momentum that is important to you and ensure that the team acts well collectively.

The idea

When taking over an existing team, you may think that you are going to be the newest person for quite a while. But the turnover of team members is often quicker than you think. There are always unexpected circumstances that lead to departures and new arrivals.

Initially you may be reluctant to see team members move on as they have much more experience than you. But while these members bring experience and knowledge, they may not share the same perspective as you. New members bring a freshness and strong desire to do well for the person who appointed them.

When new members join the team, they will need some time to get 'up to speed' in order to be fully effective. An agreed induction programme and a clear stating of initial accountabilities will help them make good progress. Some allowance will need to be made for new members, but not for long if the momentum of the team is to be maintained.

There needs to be full acceptance that new team members will learn through experience; initial misjudgements should be regarded as valuable learning rather than cause for blame. New members can therefore 'jump on board' confidently – encouraged, supported and challenged by the rest of the team.

Jeff ensured that his new team members had effective induction, after which he expected them to be pulling their own weight quickly. He was demanding of his new recruits but was willing to give them some of his time and put in place effective training and coaching support. He relied on the freshness and enthusiasm of his new appointees to take them quickly up the learning curve; he was always supportive when they were learning through tough experiences.

In practice

- Always see changes of team members as a positive rather than a negative

- Ensure proper, structured induction for all new team members

- Be demanding about the transfer of knowledge and expertise from departing to new team members

- Expect a new team member to get up to speed on the essentials quickly

- Put in place development and coaching arrangements to enable them to step up effectively

- Be explicitly open to fresh perspectives and ideas from new team members

19 KNOW WHO YOUR ALLIES ARE

WHEN TAKING OVER an existing team, you need to be clear who are your allies and supporters and how best to build up their number and influence.

The idea

The governance arrangements may have set out the relationship between different team members, about when they are individually accountable and when they are accountable as part of a team. The commitment of individuals to the success of the whole team is needed, whatever the formal governance structure might be.

The reality is that the degree of support for you will vary. Some will be delighted that you have been appointed and want to contribute fully to your success. Others may be only partial in their support because of a touch of resentment about their not having been appointed to the role, or because they are frustrated in some way or another. They may need some time to be convinced that you are the right appointee.

Being clear who your allies are at an emotional level is important. You may have a natural rapport with some people, or a shared set of values, which means they are committed to your success.

Sometimes building allies is about recognising what is the experience and development that they stand to gain from interacting with you and the wider team. Recognising the potential of individuals and creating a situation where they can learn and be more confident can have an immediate payback in their wanting to be a strong supporter and ally of yours.

Your allies might be at both senior and junior levels. Those people who are working in support of the team will often see it as an objective to enable you to take your priorities forward. The ideal is a network of allies who will give you frank advice and with whom there can be complete openness and trust. It is then a matter of gradually winning over those who are neutral or sceptical.

Be wary of those you think are seeking to undermine you. You might be seeing concerns where they don't exist, hence the importance of having evidence over a reasonable period before drawing a conclusion that someone does not have your best interests at heart. The best course of action then might be an open discussion with the individual, in which you seek their perspective on the priorities of the team and the working relationship. One possibility might be to have a three-way discussion involving a team coach.

A key consideration is not to let suspicions about a lack of commitment fester for too long. If someone does act as if you are taking the team in the wrong direction, it certainly requires open and frank discussion. It might mean that it is time for them to move on, with appropriate recognition for their past contributions.

Jeff knew that he would always get frank advice from one of his team members whom he knew well from previous roles, and from a couple of younger people who had worked for him at an earlier stage. He knew he had to work closely with some of the other team members to understand their concerns and build areas of joint commitment before they changed from being neutral to becoming more positive about what he was seeking to do.

Jeff also recognised that a couple of the team members who had been there for five years were ingrained in their approach and were always going to bring a degree of scepticism. He had to decide how much time he was prepared to spend turning them into allies, or whether he should instead encourage them to apply for other roles.

In practice

- Recognise who your allies are and listen to their perspectives

- Identify how you can enable team members to develop their careers so that they move from being neutral to being supportive of you

- Recognise who is sceptical about you and be open with them in discussion in order to understand their concerns

- Be willing to invest time in people so that they are more confident that you are taking the team in the right direction

- Seek ways to enable sceptics to move on with honour

20 BE WILLING TO MAKE HARD DECISIONS

THERE WILL BE HARD DECISIONS to make about priorities, processes and people – taking them well is essential for your credibility.

The idea

There are few things more dispiriting than seeing newly appointed leaders seeking to prove themselves by making a sequence of quick decisions that bear no relation to each other. Leaders unsure of themselves can fall into the trap of thinking they have to make quick decisions to justify their appointment.

As a new team leader, asking questions and listening well while playing back your developing understanding is a proven way of building credibility. But sometimes hard decisions have to be made. A decision may have been left for your arrival. Someone might be so put out by your appointment that they are not pulling their weight. There may be financial constraints with hard decisions on prioritisation waiting to be made. When an early decision is required, there needs to be clarity in communicating the reasons, with evidence about the necessity for such a decision.

You may feel that you are making hard decisions with only limited evidence and experience, but sometimes there is a trade-off between the need for an early decision and your becoming fully acquainted with all the background and considerations. When a hard decision needs to be taken, you need to decide who you can discuss it with so you triangulate the issue and get a perspective from a source you trust. An external mentor or coach can help you crystallise your thoughts so you are clear about your rationale and how you will handle concerned or critical reactions.

Jeff knew that he had to take some hard decisions early on about terminating a couple of projects which had not delivered over a couple of years, even though there were always reasons why more time was needed. Jeff initiated a quick review about cost-effectiveness against a set of criteria, which gave him clear evidence that these two projects should come to an end. Though he had to have painful conversations with the relevant team leaders, Jeff's credibility across the team rose significantly as he demonstrated that he was willing to tackle this issue which his predecessors had failed to address fully.

In practice

- Recognise that when you take over a team you often have to take hard decisions

- Set clear timescales for collecting evidence

- Prepare carefully for frank conversations with your evidence ready

- Recognise that it is part of your job to take decisions that some will find painful, and not to put these decisions off

- Be clear who are the trusted individuals with whom you can talk through hard decisions

- Recognise how you relate hard decisions to the values that are most important to you

SECTION C
BRINGING OUT THE BEST IN TEAM MEMBERS

21 KNOW THEIR PREFERENCES AND WHAT KEEPS THEM FRESH AT WORK

IF YOU KNOW THE PREFERENCES of individual team members and understand what keeps them fresh and motivated at work, you can more readily draw out their qualities and energy.

The idea

Knowing the preferred thinking and working styles of your team helps you to steer their thinking and energy in a constructive way. The use of psychometric tools such as MBTI can create a constructive picture in your mind and that of other team members about how an individual thinks and makes decisions.

For instance, if you recognise that some members of your team are 'reflectors', it helps you pace the way ideas are developed so that there is opportunity between meetings for individuals to think through the implications of particular courses of action. Where you see members who prefer to talk ideas through, you can give them space to discuss and think aloud in order for them to reach conclusions.

When members of a team understand each other's preferences, they more readily make allowance for different ways of thinking and working. As team leader, you have a responsibility to encourage people to operate 'out of preference', so that they are able to engage effectively with colleagues who work differently.

When you lead a team, it will normally be obvious to you when energy levels rise and when they fall. You may sometimes feel caught by the vagaries of other people's moods. Being attentive to what is making a team energetic and fresh in its interaction, and what dampens or kills that interaction, is a key part of good leadership. You want to develop a team that is mature enough to recognise that to keep fresh and effective its members need to deploy their preferences, and act effectively out of preference.

Jeanette was the leader of a large science department in a pharmaceutical firm. Some of her team leaders were scientists while others had a commercial focus, seeking to develop the scientific work commercially. The scientists tended to be reflectors while the commercial people were more extroverted in their style. There was a risk of the two groups acting in their own silos.

Jeanette asked a qualified practitioner to take all the team members through MBTI Step II, which gave an analysis that provided a rich basis for discussion – individually and as a team. The ensuing discussions helped the members of the team to understand their respective preferences when doing long-term planning or making decisions. They developed a greater understanding of when they relied on factual evidence and when they used emotional awareness to best effect.

In practice

- Observe team members to understand their preferences and what keeps them fresh at work

- Use psychometric tools selectively to bring insights and then promote open discussion based on this data

- Encourage people to be confident in using their preferences to best effect

- Create situations where team members are acting out of preference – this as an important part of their development

22 RECOGNISE THE TYPE OF LEADERSHIP THEY NEED FROM YOU

You MAY HAVE a preferred approach to leading, but bringing out the best in a team means recognising the type of leadership it needs from you.

The idea

When you have taken on leadership of a team, you will want to understand the team members' expectations of you. However, what your team wants from you may not be what they need.

After initial conversations and observations, you will reach a view about the type of leadership they need. Their initial comments to you might be that they want firm, directive leadership, but your perspective might be that this is the last thing they need. You see the risk of the team becoming too dependent upon you, with their effectiveness being inhibited by their wanting to be told what to do. You may judge that what the team really needs from you is help building its confidence and assertiveness.

When judging what type of leadership a team needs, there is a necessary process of creating a conversation drawing out their perspectives, while having an evolving picture in your mind about what is needed.

Sometimes the leadership that a team needs is for you to be present and supportive, and not to say or do much. When I was a member of leadership teams in my 30s, I gained most from those leaders who gave me space to grow and offered a very limited number of steering prompts. Anything more directive would have been debilitating rather than stimulating. I needed to learn through my own endeavours and my own mistakes.

The team leaders said to Jeanette that they wanted her to be a public support for the work they did and to ensure they had adequate resources. Their signals were that they wanted Jeanette to keep a distance. Jeanette recognised this desire for independence of thought and action, but was clear in her own mind that what the team leaders needed was a greater sense of shared purpose. There needed to be stronger understanding and links between the scientists and the commercial teams.

Jeanette articulated clearly what she observed about limited communications and got grudging acceptance that there was an issue. Gradually, through hearing what Jeanette observed, the team leaders accepted that the issue had to be addressed. Once they accepted the need for change, she gave them the responsibility to specify what needed to be done differently going forward and how best to establish stronger cross-departmental working.

In practice

- Listen to what team members say about the type of leadership they want and seek to understand why they are expressing those views

- Do your own thinking about the type of leadership they need

- Where there is a divergence between what team members want and what you think they need, be willing to encourage open conversation about the leadership you might bring

- Allow your thinking about what the team needs from you to evolve, but do not be brow-beaten into submission

23 ENSURE EFFECTIVE RECOGNITION

Most team members will welcome recognition from you even if they are not actively seeking it.

The idea

The strongest and most independent members of your team are still human. They may not look as if they need praise and recognition, but most human beings respond well to positive feedback.

Effective recognition is not about general platitudes but specific comments on actions and contributions that made a difference. The more you are able to recognise the contribution of an individual to the effectiveness of the whole team, the greater will be the reinforcement of good practice and the cooperation across the team as a whole.

When I am working with a team, I periodically ask team members to be explicit in their appreciation of individual colleagues. I might suggest, in a plenary conversation, that each team member says what they most appreciate about the contribution of the person on their left.

Alternatively, I might invite team members to pair up with a colleague and say what they most appreciate about each other's contribution. I then repeat this process with different pairings. The result often is team members commenting that they had not realised how others viewed their contribution. The point is not about self-satisfaction; it is about the pleasure of realising that your contribution is appreciated.

Jeanette saw the team leaders as committed to their work and determined to ensure good outcomes. She praised the team for its professional standards. When she had got the team leaders to a point where they were working more closely in partnership together, Jeanette talked openly about the shift in their approach and the benefits of their joint working.

Jeanette appreciated that she needed to talk up the success of the teams in the way they worked together in order to reinforce the attitudes and behaviour that she judged essential going forward. Jeanette used praise as a valuable leadership tool. This was not false flattery; it was targeted reinforcement of constructive dialogue and prioritisation. Jeanette was persistent in praising and recognising the joint working both inside and outside the organisation. The team leaders knew and accepted that these were the working practices and behaviours that Jeanette was seeking to reinforce.

In practice

- Look for opportunities to recognise the contributions people have made

- Be specific in the words you use so that the hearer understands what in particular you are recognising

- Seek to recognise and reinforce good practice in the way team members work together

- Recognise the joint contribution of team members in the comments you make to your own boss and to leaders in other related organisations

- Keep repeating words of recognition; do not feel you only need to say them once

24 RESPECT WHAT GIVES THEM ENERGY IN OTHER SPHERES

IT IS IMPORTANT TO understand what gives team members energy outside the team and the interrelationship between their energy levels in the various spheres.

The idea

When I lead a workshop, I often ask the participants, 'What has given you energy outside work in recent weeks?' This always leads to an interesting mix of responses, with laughter and teasing breaking through. The responses often lead to people being surprised at what other people are engaged with. There is a brightness and freshness in their contributions, which then infuses the atmosphere of the workshop.

Some people describe individual pursuits, while others refer to their participation in a sports team or in a community or faith-based activity. When someone talks of team activities giving them energy, it gives clues about the type of team contribution they might make going forward.

Once you know what gives energy to individuals in other spheres, there is a golden opportunity to draw out the relevance of that learning and encourage them to keep up these other activities. When a team is busy and going through tough times, encourage team members to keep doing activities that enable them to renew their energy. If someone under pressure ceases to go to a team or group event that is special to them, they might be creating a new problem rather than solving the presenting issue of lack of time.

Jeanette discovered that one of her team leaders played an active role in a tennis club while another was treasurer at their local church. They both found fulfilment in these activities. Jeanette invited them to talk about how these activities energised them and what lessons they drew from the committee running the tennis club or the parochial church council that were relevant to leading well in the pharmaceutical company.

Because Jeanette tapped into these personal interests, she was able to recognise the importance of these activities as sources of energy for these colleagues. When she invited the two leaders to talk about these parallel experiences, other members of the team became more conscious of the value of being engaged in team activities outside work.

In practice

- Invite team members to share experiences about what gives them energy outside work, particularly in terms of what type of contribution to a team energises them

- Encourage them to continue with activities that give them energy outside work, especially when there is pressure at work

- Encourage team members to take up new interests and drop older activities in order to help ensure activities outside work renew energy and do not begin to sap it

25 KNOW WHAT YOU WILL DO IF THEY DO NOT DELIVER

BEING CLEAR IN YOUR MIND how you will address a situation when team members do not deliver is important, so you do not get diverted by the emotions of the relationship.

The idea

Bringing out the best in team members is about focused encouragement and enabling them to grow in confidence and competence. Good-quality challenge is part of enabling people to grow and develop in a fruitful direction.

Sometimes hard messages will need to be sent. Expectations will have been set and a programme of work agreed. If someone is not delivering their part in the agreement, there will be a need for thoughtful discussion about what has gone wrong and why. You will want to give people the opportunity to continue to learn and develop, and move forward.

Setting explicit expectations about the contribution of team members to the overall enterprise is important. You can make explicit that their performance assessment will include how effectively they support other members of the team and contribute to the outcomes the team is seeking to achieve. Where someone is letting their team members down, it is not fair to their colleagues to allow the situation to continue without intervention. If, following encouragement and good-quality development opportunities, one of your team is not developing in the way you expect, then a hard conversation is inevitable.

It can be helpful to think through in advance when you take over the leadership of a team how you would handle a situation if someone is not delivering. You want to bring an objectivity in looking at the evidence and a dispassionate approach that recognises an individual's personal circumstances but does not let that override the needs of the whole team. You will want to enable someone to move on with honour, but move on they must.

Jeanette was conscious that a team leader in one of the science areas always looked grumpy. He was the last person to volunteer to share in any corporate work. He led a couple of pieces of work on behalf of the whole team which drifted away with no outcomes. Jeanette was frank with this individual about her concerns and set clear expectations for the following three months. There was limited progress in this period both in the individual's direct area of responsibility and in his contributions to the team as a whole. Jeanette felt she had given the individual adequate forewarning and the opportunity to contribute more fully.

Eventually Jeanette expressed an expectation that this individual move on within six months. She organised outplacement support and was willing to recommend pay in lieu of notice. Jeanette was clear that she was not going to be taken advantage of any more and that the presence of the individual in the team was having a negative effect on the overall effectiveness and morale of the team.

In practice

- Be objective in assessing who is delivering and who is not delivering

- Be explicit in the feedback when someone is not delivering and listen to their reasons and explanation

- Be willing to give a second chance, but keep an eye on whether progress is being made

- When you have a plan for responding to someone who is not delivering, don't deviate from that plan unless there are very good reasons to do so

- Be mindful about the effect on the overall team when someone is not delivering

- Be willing to push hard on letting go of team members if they are having a counter-productive effect over a significant period

26 ENABLE PEOPLE TO HAVE THEIR VOICE

WHEN YOU ENABLE PEOPLE to have their voice, they become more confident and influential.

The idea

As a team leader, you can often forget what it was like to be a new member. You have left behind your hesitation about contributing in new situations. For many people, joining a new team can be daunting, with hesitation stilling them into silence. Enabling someone to have their voice is about welcoming them, recognising they have a part to play, encouraging them to comment, welcoming their contribution, encouraging others to listen, and enabling them to influence the flow of the conversation.

Most people are part of a team for a reason, so they carry the expectation that they contribute from a particular perspective. But as you get to know the members of your team, you will be conscious of the breadth of their experience and how they might contribute in a wider range of areas. Your role as team leader is to encourage individuals to speak up and contribute from right across their experience.

Enabling people to have their voice includes promoting dialogue where people can build on each other's contributions and develop a set of interrelated reasons for taking a particular course of action. Enabling people to have their voice is also about giving them the legitimacy to push back if they regard a particular course of action as misconceived.

Jeanette recognised that she had been setting clear expectations for her team. There was a risk that they were in 'compliant acquiescent' mode. They would talk about scientific things but were reluctant to contribute when wider corporate business issues were discussed. Jeanette knew that she needed to catch the imagination of her team leaders about what might be possible going forward.

Jeanette arranged a half day with the team away from the office. This change of environment loosened them up. Sitting in a circle and with no table in the middle, the team leaders became franker about their aspirations and hopes for the future. Jeanette encouraged this greater openness. She used questions to prompt conversation and summarised next steps rather than forcing any particular conclusions.

In practice

- Recognise when members of your team are particularly quiet and seek to understand why

- Set up conversations away from the main work area to prompt more reflective conversation

- Encourage team members to say what is most important to them and demonstrate you have been listening to what has been said

- Recognise that some people, when they join a team, can feel inhibited; seek deliberately to draw them out in conversation

- Promote dialogue as a means of enabling different voices to be heard

- Use the power of the summary to crystallise what has been said and to move action forward

BE A GOOD COACH

A CRUCIAL SKILL as a team leader is using a coaching approach effectively to draw out the capabilities of those working for and with you.

The idea

In a fast-moving world, coaching skills are an essential pre-requisite of leadership and management. They are not an optional extra. The good leader will use a range of coaching approaches to try to catch the imagination of members of their team about what is possible and bring out the best in them.

Using a coaching approach well as a team leader depends on you being willing to stand back and not always be in direct control. Success comes through enabling others to review and reframe their contribution, and to be refocused and re-energised.

Using a coaching approach can be a liberating experience as a team leader. It will release you from feeling you have to solve every problem yourself. Applying a coaching approach is demanding, but in a very different way. Your ability to ask the right questions and bring different insights becomes more important than finding an instant solution.

Bringing out the best in others through a coaching approach will enable you to bring out the best in yourself. What is it 'only you can do' to ensure the success of a particular endeavour?

Being a good coach of your team involves seeing questions as the key that unlocks, bringing a focus on facts, being realistic about possibilities and leaving lots of space for reflection. Coaching members of your team involves listening to their emotions as well as their words, and understanding their motivations. Good coaches trust their intuition about when to intervene with members of their team, when to ask questions and when to focus conversations on what somebody has learnt rather than what they are going to do next.

Jeanette was conscious that some of her team leaders were ready for more coaching-type interactions. They had turned the corner in terms of motivation. They wanted the team to be successful and saw the scope for more effective bilateral working. They were reaching out to their colleagues more. Jeanette used a gentle but purposeful coaching approach with them as individuals and with the team as a whole.

Jeanette got the team to reflect on how more mutual listening and engagement had developed. She invited members of the team to contribute thoughts about what they might do to further build on this momentum. Jeanette moved from focused interventions about forward action to more open questions about what team members thought should be done next. Using this approach took the momentum of constructive change to the next level.

In practice

- Experiment with using a coaching approach more often
- Observe when a more questioning, reflective tone works in enabling team members to be clearer about next steps
- Use a coaching approach with both individual members of the team and with the team as a whole
- Be open to doing some training to further develop your coaching skills and repertoire

28 ENCOURAGE TEAM MEMBERS TO WORK IN COLLABORATION RATHER THAN COMPETITION

IF YOU ENCOURAGE team members to collaborate rather than compete with each other, the team is likely to be more effective, with less risk of friction and dysfunction.

The idea

A seemingly attractive way of generating progress is to rely on the competitive element between team members so they are striving to do better than each other. Most reward and recognition arrangements are based on competition as a driver. But if you set a tone of collaboration and partnership, you are laying down a course which is more likely to lead to harmonious and constructive outcomes.

Some individuals thrive on competition. But once you have 'beaten' a fellow team member, trust is eroded and the likelihood of effective joint working in the future diminishes. Being competitive might have a short-term gain but will lead to long-term pain.

Being collaborative is not about pooling weakness or applying the lowest common denominator. As team leader you may set a clear expectation about members of the team working together to deliver significant changes. You are likely to want to share examples of where collaboration has worked effectively and where the outcome of joint working has been 'more than the sum of the parts'.

Effective collaboration for a team is both within the team and with other parts of the wider organisation, as well as with external bodies. If you want collaboration to be part of the culture of your organisation, you need to demonstrate its value. If you are seen to collaborate and build common cause with others, this will be regarded as approved behaviour, with others then seeking to emulate you. Role-modelling effective collaboration is the best way of ensuring your team members focus on collaboration rather than competition.

Jeanette saw the risk of her science and commercial directors working with an element of competition between them. Rationally they knew they needed to co-operate in order to maximise the effectiveness of the business, but emotionally there was a difference between the approaches of the scientific and the commercial specialists. Jeanette set clear expectations about working together on joint activities. She praised and recognised effective collaboration whenever she saw it. She came down hard on unwarranted competition and any sniping between teams.

In practice

- Notice, describe and praise good collaboration when you see it

- Be explicit about when your expectations are collaboration, and when competition with a different organisation is a necessary part of the team delivering

- Encourage collaboration at a range of levels

- Recognise that collaboration has to have both a rational and an emotional element if it is to work well

- Accept that it takes time for leaders in two organisations to work effectively in collaboration with each other

29 BALANCE FACE-TO-FACE AND VIRTUAL COMMUNICATION

THE RIGHT COMBINATION of face-to-face and virtual communication will differ over time depending on preferences and needs. Choices that maximise the effectiveness of communication need to be made.

The idea

We may have a preference for face-to-face communication but at the same time recognise that using virtual communication well is essential. Virtual communication provides a means of sharing information and ideas at short notice. A brief reflection in a text or e-mail can unblock an issue and allow new thinking to move forward. But an abrupt text or e-mail can stifle dialogue and send people back into their bunkers.

Virtual communication is increasingly important as teams become more global and more dispersed. Gone are the days when members of a leadership team are in the same building five days a week and able to rely solely on face-to-face communication. An effective team needs to develop its way of using video conferencing, Skype meetings and telephone conferences to best effect.

Electronic communication is an excellent means of keeping team members up to speed but can be a dangerous way of trying to work through complicated issues on which there are strongly held views. A good team leader knows when to pull an issue into discussion rather than relying on further e-mail exchanges. A good team leader uses electronic communication selectively as a way of gleaning views from right across an organisation, and then communicating what the senior team has concluded and why.

Jeanette saw it as helpful that her staff were located on a limited number of sites. She wanted to encourage face-to-face dialogue as much as possible, but did not want to put in place heavy expectations about regular face-to-face meetings. She placed strong emphasis on having in the diary workshop-type events when the team could be reflective. She saw face-to-face conversation as essential for those meetings.

Jeanette often arranged for meetings that were more about information-sharing to be conducted by telephone or Skype, emphasising that she was doing this in order to be time-efficient. She talked about the limitations of different approaches and encouraged team leaders to talk through both the benefits and limitations. As a result of fruitful exchanges, the team got into a better equilibrium about when face-to-face was essential and when it was desirable.

In practice

- Do not assume that face-to-face communication is necessarily better than virtual: they each have a place if used well

- Be explicit about varying the way you use face-to-face meetings so some have a brisk business agenda, while others are more reflective in considering longer-term plans and aspirations

- See it as your responsibility to set the tone about the right balance between different forms of communication

- Develop the skill of using text messaging in a supportive and measured way

- Recognise that as team members change, the preferred balance in the communication arrangements will evolve

30 RECOGNISE WHEN YOU NEED TO BE UNREASONABLE

BEING UNREASONABLE – provided it is within the realms of the doable – can stimulate individuals and teams to be far more effective than they would have thought possible.

The idea

An eminent leader once told me that sometimes a good leader has to be unreasonable in their requests. When a team is facing a crisis, the leader is going to be making demands on the team far in excess of normal expectations. The leader will be explaining that the circumstances dictate the need for this type of response. Team members will accept the requirement for long hours and sustained effort in a crisis.

On other occasions, a team leader may regard it as essential to set a strict timetable or an objective that has not been attained before. But such requests must be based on evidence about what is doable. If a team has walked six miles in three hours, it is probably not an unreasonable request for them to walk seven miles in the next three hours. The extra distance is a stretch but stays within the bounds of the achievable.

Sometimes a leader may not have firm evidence that a goal is attainable, but by encouraging the team to look at progress step by step, a momentum can be created whereby the seemingly impossible becomes doable, as a result of careful preparation.

When it becomes clear that your team needs to deliver on a demanding timescale, a judgement needs to be made about whether you describe what needs to be done in a measured, progressive way, or whether you acknowledge that a request or timescale is at the boundary of reasonableness, with particular thought needing to be given to how the task can be tackled in an innovative way.

As a team leader, there will be times when you will need to go beyond what you regard as reasonable. But linked with such requests will always be a careful explanation of why, and the intent to provide people with the tools they need to do the job and the emotional support essential to keep up motivation.

Jeanette was determined to bring together the expertise of the scientists and those with commercial experience, as there was a clear opportunity to exploit some of the latest scientific progress commercially. She set tight deadlines for this work to be taken forward. She acknowledged that the timescale might be unreasonable, but also set out cogent reasons why it was worth striving to achieve. Although initially met with scepticism, Jeanette had marshalled her evidence well and knew how to motivate her team members; the tight deadline was within the bounds of the doable, and released new energy within the team.

In practice

- Draw lessons from how others have made unreasonable requests in a crisis and motivated people effectively

- Be mindful how you explain requests that will be regarded by some as unreasonable

- Measure what is possible based on what has happened before

- Be willing to make unreasonable demands of yourself too, so that you are seen to be part of the same set of expectations

- Recognise when apparently unreasonable requests have been delivered effectively

BUILDING A NEW TEAM

31 BE CLEAR ON OUTCOMES TO BE DELIVERED AND THE TONE TO BE SET

A NEW TEAM WILL COHERE much more readily if there is clarity about outcomes to be delivered and the right tone is set from the beginning.

The idea

Sometimes the outcomes for the work of a team are clear: e.g. a project has to be completed or a design formulated. On other occasions, the outcomes may be more aspirational: a group of teachers may be designing a curriculum to help raise the performance of students.

No matter how excited team members might be at the outset, their enthusiasm can be dissipated if there is a dissonance between the outcomes they want to see delivered and those of other participants in the team. A starting point for any team is to think through and discuss the outcomes they aspire to.

Whether the outcomes are predetermined by you as the team leader or jointly developed, there is always scope to work through questions about how the outcomes are to be delivered. As the team leader, you want to set a tone without dictating the precise way in which the team will operate. Elements of the tone might be about the balance between why, what and how. You will want to set out a clear prospectus about *why* the team has been brought together; *what* the team is there for; and *how* the team can work together, for example by setting out expectations about listening to and engaging with each other.

James had been appointed to lead a team which would oversee the design and implementation of a major IT system. He recognised that the first task was to be clear about the specification to ensure there was no ambiguity about the outcome to be delivered. He made some early appointments to the team – people who could assist him in developing clarity about the specification. As team members were appointed, he ensured that the specification was understood and regularly referred to. He knew from past experience how easy it was for team members to fixate on one aspect of the specification and not see the whole picture.

James also recognised that he needed to set the right tone for the team. He wanted to ensure the right balance between focus and adaptability. He wanted people to listen to and engage with each other and the client, whilst at the same time keeping the end point in view so they were not distracted from the ultimate outcomes. James helped set the tone by sharing examples of previous projects that had worked well or less well. He got new team members to talk through their expectations and share examples of effective teams that they had been members of.

In practice

- Be willing to spend time on defining outcomes

- Be relentless in trying to build as clear a specification as possible; ensure it is written down and understood by all those with a direct interest

- Be clear and consistent about the tone you set

- Share stories of where this tone has led to constructive outcomes and be uninhibited in repeating those stories

- Invite new team members to share their stories about the relationship between the tone and the resulting outcomes

32 BE CLEAR ON THE BALANCE OF SKILLS THAT ARE NEEDED

TEAMS WORK EFFECTIVELY if there is a balance of both technical and engagement skills.

The idea

A football team needs to include people with a mix of skills. Some players are good at defending and others at attacking; some are more effective on the left-hand side of the pitch and others on the right-hand side. A goalkeeper brings a different set of skills from a forward.

The football team is not just dependent on the skills of the players on the field. The full team includes those with managerial skills, the technical coaches, the medical staff and those who look after the players' kit.

On the field, good players draw out the skills of their colleagues through the way they pass the ball. A midfielder in possession of the ball anticipates his teammates' movements, so the ball can be passed to the foot of the winger running energetically towards the goal line.

A sports team provides a useful analogy for any team. When selecting a new team, you are looking for a range of technical skills that in combination add up to the expertise you want. But you are also looking for skills of working together well, anticipating the unpredictable, engaging effectively with other members of the team, being resilient in times of pressure, and bouncing back when things go badly. It can be helpful to use the sporting team analogy to help crystallise the mix of technical and relational skills that are going to be necessary for the team to excel. Defining a clear set of expectations and writing those down can then become a useful check-list as you begin to appoint team members.

James needed a mix of technical IT skills within his team, but he was also conscious that team members needed to be able to work together well and draw out the best in each other. When he talked with potential recruits, he sought to understand how they had engaged with colleagues and clients, and how they had handled tough moments. James was particularly interested in how prospective team members had handled setbacks, and the level of adaptability, courage and resilience they had shown in such circumstances.

In practice

- Think through the mix of skills that makes a sports team successful

- Think of the balance of skills that have led to success in teams doing similar tasks to the one you are setting up

- List the technical skills you seek and commit time to searching out people who have those skills

- Identify the relationship, adaptability and resilience skills that you need and assess potential members against these criteria

- Be clear what weighting you give to different types of skills, e.g. how prepared are you to accept a team member who is technically very good but limited in engagement skills?

- Resist the temptation to appoint the first available person in order to get the project going: you might appoint in haste and regret at leisure

33 BE CLEAR ABOUT THE VALUES UNDERPINNING THE TEAM

CLARITY ABOUT THE VALUES underpinning a team provides a benchmark against which actions can be assessed and discussed.

The idea

The Scottish Prison Service recently developed a set of core values, which staff across the organisation contributed to defining:

Belief   We believe people can change

Respect   We have proper regard for people, their needs and their human rights

Integrity   We apply high ethical, moral and professional standards

Openness   We work with others to achieve the best standards

Courage   We have the courage to care regardless of circumstances

Humility   We cannot do this on our own; we recognise we can learn from others

The organisation describes the importance of these values in the following terms: 'Living by strong values, consistent with the unique nature of responsibilities of our business, will be key to delivering our mission and are at the heart of every decision we make'. The leadership team is seeking to apply these values both across the whole organisation and in the way the senior team operates.

It is very helpful for a senior team to define four to six key words which sum up the values they seek to apply both within the organisation and in the way they work themselves. For values to be effective, there need to be periodic moments when there is a conversation about the extent to which the values are applied.

Take one value at a time and reflect on its relevance to actions and attitudes over the preceding or forthcoming months.

When a team is working out what approach to take on a complicated issue, it helps to view that issue through the lens of individual values, so as to cast light on the most appropriate next steps.

Once his team was in place, James arranged an away day to discuss the values that the team wanted to apply going forward. He invited team members to come to the event having thought through the four or five key values they considered most important. He began by putting members of the team in pairs to share these values and to agree, as a pair, what were the five key values going forward.

James then asked pairs to combine into groups of four, work through the different suggestions, and agree a set of five values that they believed would be most important for the team to be successful. There were then four presentations by four groups of four people. This led to an open debate with five core values chosen. James as team leader steered the discussion away from a couple of values which he did not think were as important as others, but was happy to go with the main thrust of the conversation and became a strong advocate of the agreed set of five values.

In practice

- Create time for values to be discussed

- Read up on examples of values that have been used by different teams and how they have been applied successfully

- Think through how you want to use values as a means of reviewing actions and assessing prospective decisions

- Ensure there is full engagement with members in the selection of key values

34 RECOGNISE POTENTIAL DE-RAILERS

IF A POTENTIAL DE-RAILER is recognised and planned for, it is much less likely to disrupt the momentum of a team.

The idea

It is always worth investing time thinking through what are the key risks and what are the de-railers that may throw you off course. A risk anticipated and prepared for is going to be more straightforward to deal with than a risk that comes unexpectedly.

A clinical look at potential de-railers will mean that they are examined carefully and dispassionately. Some de-railers can at first glance look devastating. But once thought has been given to contingency plans, the most acute of potential crises will seem more manageable.

One risk might be losing key staff, hence the importance of succession planning. Another risk might be that a lot hangs on a single customer relationship, hence the importance of developing complementary relationships with other members of the customer team. There might be a risk about timescales, hence the value of investing time in examining where current timescales could be shortened, or where they could be made more secure. There may be a risk of key data not being available by a particular time, hence the importance of working with the suppliers of that data well before the due date to ensure that any problems are worked through.

A key indication of the openness of a team is whether participants feel inhibited about mentioning potential risks or de-railers. Effective teams create an atmosphere where people feel able to talk of risks and de-railers at an early stage, with time being set aside to work through the causes and consequences. One of the most valuable contributions to any team is the ability to spot a risk early and to encourage thoughtful and constructive conversation about how such a risk is tackled.

James was conscious that the IT project was working to a tight timescale. He recognised that it was important to be positive about the doability of the project to build motivation within the team. But James also knew a rigorous look at risks and de-railers was essential. He set aside time for an early discussion. He invited specific team members to take accountability for reviewing named risks and designing how best to address those risks. The team scored the likelihood and potential impact of each risk and then reviewed those scores on a regular basis.

When a key member of the team became ill, the confidence of the team was not diminished because they had already thought through this type of eventuality. Responsibilities within the team were adapted and another person brought in on a temporary basis. The momentum was not lost because the team had a plan they could readily implement.

In practice

- Set aside time for risks and de-railers to be looked at
- Provide time for risks and de-railers to be worked through carefully and dispassionately
- Invest in contingency planning and be ready to demonstrate that the contingency planning is worthwhile
- Give recognition to people who identify risks and de-railers and put in place actions to circumvent the de-railers and keep up the team's momentum

35 BRING BOTH REALISM AND ASPIRATION

STRIKING A REASONABLE BALANCE between realism and aspiration is essential to the ultimate success of any team.

The idea

Being positive means believing that no matter how intractable a challenge appears, there is a way out. Progress for a team comes from focusing on what can be done going forward and not becoming completely preoccupied with what went wrong.

A lesson from working as a coach with senior leaders in many different spheres and countries is the importance of leaders having grounded optimism rather than false optimism. Grounded optimism requires a constructive mindset combined with a healthy realism about what is happening. It demands looking at the evidence and facts clearly and dispassionately. Realism involves seeking reality, digging deeper if you are uneasy, being relentless in getting to the bottom of issues but always keeping a watchful eye on where you are aiming to get to, and remembering the rationale that is keeping you going forward and the progress that is being made.

Good decisions are based on a realism about data, finances, perceptions and politics, but it is always worth coming back to the aspiration and asking yourself questions like 'How have we moved mountains before?', 'What can we do to build a stronger support for this aspiration?' and 'What can we do as a next step to provide evidence that this aspiration is attainable?'

When you see people in your team who are at risk of 'putting their head in the sand', be alert to this and be ready to encourage, cajole or persuade them out of this restrictive mode of thinking.

James was very conscious of the different starting points for the members of his team. Some focused on the aspirational while others were at risk of getting bogged down with a limited view on what was realistic. James needed to keep them talking to each other. He was explicit about the language of realism and aspiration, inviting people to talk through their perspectives using these two words, focusing on how to maintain an appropriate balance. He knew that he needed to be optimistic and keep pushing the boundaries forward.

In practice

- Seek to bring grounded optimism to the way you lead your team

- Encourage realism and honesty about evidence and data

- Always keep the aspirational in view and keep repeating messages about aspiration, populating the messages with up-to-date evidence

- Recognise that the balance between realism and aspiration is likely to be different for different people

- Adapt your approach when you talk with individual team members, being clear what catches their imagination and what motivates them going forward

- When someone is 'putting their head in the sand', be direct in what you say to them

36 TREAT YOUR TEAM MEMBERS AS IF THEY ARE VOLUNTEERS

If you view every member of your team as a volunteer, you will be able to think more clearly about how to motivate them to make willing and effective contributions.

The idea

There is a risk of dividing people into two groups – those who are employed and those who are volunteers – as well as a false assumption that employees are willing to be told what to do, while volunteers need to be motivated. The truth is not so straightforward. The productivity and creativity of paid team members will fluctuate just as much as the productivity and creativity of volunteers. Both need to be motivated and recognised for their individual qualities.

The leader working with a group of volunteers recognises the importance of encouragement, praise and thanks. Volunteers need to be recognised or they will walk away. Many effective leaders have learnt their leadership skills through working with volunteers and have trained themselves to be fulsome in praise and recognition and able to adapt roles in order to motivate volunteers.

Transferring approaches that worked with volunteers into working with a team of paid members can be well worthwhile. Where someone is leading a team of employees, one way of developing their skills further is to take on leadership of a group of volunteers. The consequence is that the leader rapidly gains a wider repertoire of ways to motivate team members.

Treating people as volunteers does not mean ignoring performance that is less than needed. Honesty in assessing performance is equally important. It just means a wider range of approaches will be needed to influence someone to 'up their game'.

It can sometimes be helpful to invite a team to discuss how they would relate to each other if they were all volunteers. Such a discussion can bring out a greater sensitivity to the needs and preferences of others and the most effective way of building joint working. It can be helpful in a team conversation to ask each team member to respond to the question, 'If I was here as a volunteer and did not need the income, what would I need from my colleagues to motivate me and bring out the best in me?'

James was conscious that the level of commitment in his team was varied. Some were utterly professional and driven and would work long hours whatever he did. Others seemed more fickle. He recognised that he needed to motivate them. Viewing them as volunteers enabled him to think through how best to do that.

James recognised that there would be regular performance reviews in which he could be explicit about the performance of these individuals, but his first approach was to seek to stretch their curiosity, grow their professionalism and develop their impact. The question, 'If they were volunteers, how would I treat them?' helped James to be more flexible in his approach. He treated it as a personal exploration to see what approaches worked best in motivating the more laid-back members of his team.

In practice

- Remember what motivates you as a volunteer
- Draw lessons from your experience in leading volunteers

- Imagine each member of your team was a volunteer and think about how best you would motivate them

- Initiate discussion within the team about how members would bring out the best in each other if they were volunteers

- Stimulate discussion in the team about viewing members of the wider organisation as volunteers and how this perspective would influence the best way of building partnerships with them

37 BE CLEAR ON THE MILESTONES TOWARDS DESIRED OUTCOMES

MILESTONES THAT BUILD CREDIBILITY about the attainability of the team's desired outcomes help to focus the work of individuals and the team as a whole.

The idea

A set of long-term outcomes is a necessary part of focusing a team's commitment and energy; intermediate milestones are an essential means of ensuring progress. Milestones do have risks attached to them: they can lead to a slowing down rather than a speeding up if some stages are relatively straightforward to deliver. They can lead to rigidity and a fixed vision about next steps.

Milestones therefore need to be accompanied by an honest review of progress and an assessment of whether the trajectory to the next milestone continues to be appropriate.

For some team members, what will motivate them is the clarity of the ultimate outcome. They do not need intermediate milestones, and may even find milestones an inhibitor to progress. For others, a sequence of defined milestones is the way they are best focused and motivated to deliver each stage effectively. For these people, recognition when reaching milestones and celebration of progress is crucial to their maintaining high levels of commitment.

James used milestones as important staging posts. When a key milestone was reached, he always ensured there was a celebration for the team. He also used milestones as a means of reviewing progress with clients, jointly marking the success, and looking at what adjustments were needed going forward to ensure the project continued to make good progress.

James widened the scope of milestones to include the personal development of members as well as the technical work of the team. He wanted team members to be continually developing their professional skills and their way of working.

James agreed a certain number of milestone dates going forward and linked those dates to internal review meetings and meetings with the client. The fact that these meetings were in the diary long in advance provided a discipline for members of his team, and a reassurance for the client that the milestone dates were being taken seriously.

In practice

- Be explicit about defining milestones but consult carefully with key people before settling them

- Recognise that different people are motivated in different ways, hence milestones will be more important for some than others

- Plan ahead to have review meetings – internal and external – at milestone points

- Build good practice into the way milestone events are handled so that they are constructive

- Build recognition and celebration into milestone events

- Be mindful when milestones inhibit progress and give an air of rigidity

38 BE CLEAR HOW THE TEAM NEEDS TO ENGAGE WITH THE WIDER ORGANISATION

TEAMS DO NOT EXIST IN ISOLATION; they need to engage with the wider organisation if they are to thrive.

The idea

Every team, in whatever sector, is engaging with other teams and with the wider organisation. It is folly for any team to regard itself as acting in isolation. When setting up a new team, it can be well worth listing which other teams there will be a relationship with, and what areas within the organisation this team needs a relationship with in order to survive and thrive. Having drawn up a list, you can assess the relative importance of these other teams and how best a relationship can be established.

Sometimes the lead needs to come from the team leader. On other occasions the link is best done by a team member with particular expertise and background. There needs to be a division of responsibilities between team members about links across the organisation and externally. Relying on one person can create over-dependence and risks if that person is not available. Many organisations will identify a couple of people as links with other key teams or parts of the organisation so that there is always someone accessible.

James was clear that he needed to be the lead person for engaging with the client organisation's Chief Executive and the Director. He needed to build a relationship with the Finance Director while ensuring that one of his team members was the main link with the Finance Department.

James was conscious that there were other teams working on similar types of IT projects. He built a relationship with the leaders of these teams. The links between teams were important in terms of keeping up with technical developments and seeing what each team was learning. They could also share insights into the needs and behaviours of customers.

James invited people from different parts of the organisation and from external organisations to speak with his team in order to build mutual awareness. James thought it important to invest in relationships in advance, as once trust and understanding had been established with good-quality engagement, differences of opinion or unexpected events could be handled in a more measured way.

In practice

- Invest time in building key relationships with other teams that are important to the success of your team

- Split up responsibilities for keeping up good-quality relationships with different members of the team

- Always ensure there are two people who can handle a relationship going forward

- Be willing to invest in team events with other teams so that there is a sharing of expertise and joint learning

- Build a picture about how other parts of the organisation view your team in order to help you develop the most effective way of interrelating across the organisation

- Recognise the importance of engagement at both technical and emotional levels

39 | BE EXPLICIT IN BUILDING TEAM RESILIENCE

THE SUCCESS OF A TEAM depends on the resilience of its members and the team as a whole.

The idea

Resilience is dependent on building personal and team resolve so that issues are faced up to squarely. Resilience also follows from thinking through risks and de-railers and putting alternative plans in place. A successful team will have an emotional strength that flows from the resilience of each of its members.

A good team leader encourages members to keep up their physical, intellectual, emotional and spiritual resilience, and share their experiences about building up and maintaining their resilience.

As team leader, you should be mindful about how you build up your team as a whole, with good connectivity between team members and good levels of mutual support. You want there to be effective challenge in the team but not in a way that generates friction and long-term disharmony.

The resilience of the team depends on its ability to anticipate upcoming issues and talk them through in advance. Team members need to feel the potential pain of a disappointment or failure and recognise how it would feel, so that they can handle adversity when it comes and move as quickly as reasonably possible into a more positive space.

A team might role-play how they would respond to criticism or different types of unexpected events. It is well worth open discussion about what might undermine a team, and how best it can build up resilience to handle shocks and disruptions.

When James interviewed prospective members of the team, he asked them how they maintained their levels of resilience. He built an understanding with each of them about how they were going to continue to do so. James got the team to reflect on what they observed in resilient teams and what lessons they were able to draw from their previous experience. He asked them to think through what type of resilience they needed going forward and how best they built that resilience into the way they worked together and how they interrelated with other organisations.

James organised an event after a few months, where they tested out how, as a team, they would respond to different scenarios. In reviewing how they performed, the team talked explicitly about their own resilience and how they were going to build it up.

In practice

- Be open with colleagues about what you need to do to build and maintain your resilience

- Encourage each team member to set time aside to build and maintain their resilience

- Share examples of teams that have been more or less resilient and why this has been the case

- Spend time as a team thinking through how to build up resilience as a team

- Create different contexts where the team's level of resilience can be tested, with lessons learnt from these experiences being built into how the team works together

40 DEMONSTRATE YOUR ON-GOING COMMITMENT TO THE TEAM

TEAM MEMBERS LOOK TO YOU to demonstrate your on-going commitment to the team. It is important to do this while maintaining objectivity about what is going on in the team.

The idea

Team members will recognise that you need to be both committed to the team and maintaining objectivity about how it is doing. They will expect you to be 'out and about' engaging with different people, bringing perspectives back into the team. They will also expect you to be at the heart of the team and sensitive to what is happening and what is the potential for the future.

Team members will want you to stand up for the team and be robust in demonstrating progress made. They will not be surprised when you give direct messages about the team's performance and areas that need to change.

Your commitment to the team is demonstrated in praise, recognition, and a focus on continuous improvement, with a belief that individual team members do make progress and difficult obstacles can be overcome.

Demonstrating your on-going commitment to the team flows from the personal as well as the professional. Recognising the personal difficulties an individual is facing builds an engagement which can take professional commitment to another level.

James knew that there would be moments when he would need to speak up firmly in support of his team if it came under criticism; he was ready and willing to do this.

James also knew that his commitment to the team would need to be shown through his focus on performance and effective delivery of elements of the project. He knew that he must not let up in demonstrating his commitment to quality outcomes and quality relationships. Commitment meant showing that he was taking responsibility, that he could give tough messages and that he was willing to make decisions when there would be winners and losers.

James was ready to take criticism on his shoulders and provide a measure of protection for his people so they could focus on getting the work to the next stage.

In practice

- Regularly articulate your commitment to the team
- Be willing to speak up on behalf of your team when there is criticism
- Demonstrate your commitment to the team through a continued focus on performance
- Be willing to lead the team in a different direction when required by external events
- Keep demonstrating through your words and actions your commitment to the on-going delivery and effectiveness of your team

BECOMING AN EVEN BETTER TEAM LEADER

41 LEARN BY EXPERIENCE AND EXPERIMENT IN DIFFERENT CONTEXTS

THE MORE YOU EXPERIMENT and learn in different contexts, the wider will be your repertoire in leading a team.

The idea

One person I work with is the Chair of a national public sector body, who is also a non-executive Director of a private sector board, and the Chair of Trustees of a charity. She deliberately took on leadership roles in different sectors, recognising that experience and learning in one sector can be transferred to other sectors. Now past the age of 60, there has been no diminution in her energy, curiosity and willingness to learn. She is always willing to talk through different ideas and approaches, and believes in continuous learning and building in best practice from one organisation into another.

A number of leaders I have coached gained hugely from taking on additional leadership roles in a different context, for instance in a voluntary-sector organisation. This equipped them to work more effectively with volunteers, to recognise the effect of tough financial constraints, to understand how to work more constructively with people with strongly held views and to build partnerships which involve compromises.

A team leader who has led project teams with clear outcomes and timetables can gain valuable experience by leading a team which is thinking through long-term ideas. The skill of leading focused, practical discussion can then be complemented by a greater ability to lead open-ended, exploratory conversations.

Saddique was the leader of an architectural practice. He had a team of experienced architects who, whilst innovative in their designs, were conservative in their work practices. Saddique knew that he had to ensure his team became more proactive in the way they worked together and with their clients. He wanted to turn their design curiosity and energy into more effective, forward thinking and engagement with a changing market.

Saddique had recently been made Chair of a local community association. He was passionate about the community but also recognised that this would give him valuable experience in motivating team members who tended to be conservative and set in their ways. Saddique recognised that he could be more adventurous in the way he stimulated radical thinking within the leadership team of the community organisation. He began to translate some of this boldness from the voluntary organisation into his leadership of the team of architects.

In practice

- Be conscious about the limitations of your experience and how it might blinker your approach

- Draw lessons from those who lead in very different contexts

- Be open to taking on a leadership role within a team doing a different activity with different constraints upon it

- Agree to lead other teams where you would get the opportunity to experiment and widen your repertoire

42 TAKE TIME OUT TO WIDEN YOUR PERSPECTIVE

VIEW THE TIME you take talking to other leaders as an investment and not an indulgence.

The idea

You have reached a particular level because of your hard work and self-discipline. You have always made the best of opportunities to take responsibility and move issues forward. You are willing to go on courses to develop your skills – provided you can see a quick return from them. You have not been able to justify taking time out to observe other leaders and see how they approach different types of issues.

You recognise that the leader who wants to continue growing will need to invest in widening their perspective. Continued development can come from attending masterclasses, doing a higher degree, reading books on leadership, and talking with other leaders about how they approached similar situations. Autobiographies of notable leaders – whether in business, sport or politics – can bring insights from different worlds about how these individuals applied their energy, creativity and drive to bring innovation and develop effective performance in themselves and others.

Ed Catmull in his book, *Creativity, Inc.*, tells the story of the growth of Pixar Animation and its merger into one business with Disney Animation. He talks about creating the right conditions for creativity alongside creating quality films that are a success at the box office. Learning from the creativity and financial realism of Ed Catmull provides an example of the learning that can come from stories told by effective leaders.

Saddique recognised that he needed to widen his perspective. He attended workshops run by his professional association and talked to leaders of other professional organisations. He read books on aspects of leadership, always seeking to hone in on two or three ideas from each book. He took time out to think through what was working well and less well and committed thinking time to develop ideas about the leadership approach he wanted to bring to the architectural practice going forward.

In practice

- See time out to learn as an investment

- Guard against the emotional reaction that time out is wasteful indulgence

- See one or two learning points as worthwhile outcomes from reflecting on the experiences and observations of others

- Vary the way you use time out, so it is a mixture of listening, reading, talking and reflecting

- Ensure that when work is busy you still plan time out in short, focused interludes

- Use time out in a reflective and open way and see what ideas germinate

- Accept that your mind first has to wander before it hones in on key themes or practical ideas

43 DO MUTUAL MENTORING

MUTUAL MENTORING is both rewarding and enjoyable if done in a way that is win-win.

The idea

Any successful relationship has to be two-way. If mutual mentoring is to be sustained, both parties need to feel it is worth their time and investment. Mutual mentoring may be between two individuals in similar types of roles. In these instances, there is little that needs to be said about the background contexts. Both parties understand the activities and the ways of making progress and decisions in similar types of organisations. The mutual mentoring in such situations is about sharing ideas and good practice. The more there can be an equal sharing of ideas both ways round the better.

Mutual mentoring can also work well when the leaders come from very different spheres. The learning here can flow from the remarkable parallels between leading people in the public, private and voluntary sectors. Success for the leader comes through using influence well, building shared agendas, learning how to reinforce and develop good performance and the most effective ways of sharing good practice. Many leadership issues are the same in any team irrespective of the sector or the level of the team in a hierarchy, hence the value of mutual mentoring.

Saddique decided it was worth doing two different types of mutual mentoring. He linked up with the head of an architectural practice in a neighbouring town. The two firms were not in direct competition so it was possible to be open in these conversations.

These mentoring conversations enabled both Saddique and his colleague to talk through how they addressed their leadership challenges of working with professionals who were set in their ways. They tested out different ideas in conversation, applied those approaches within their practices, and then shared their observations on the outcomes.

Saddique also paired up with the Chair of a community association in a different town. This mutual mentoring helped him in his role as Chair of his local community association, and widened his understanding about leading teams with single-minded people in them. Both these mutual mentoring conversations gave him valuable learning, which he applied in the way he led his architectural practice.

In practice

- Be willing to invest time in building mutual mentoring arrangements

- Recognise the value of different types of mutual mentoring, either with people in a similar sphere to yours, or with people in a very different sphere

- Ensure that the benefits are two-way

- Articulate the transferable learning that these conversations give you

- Recognise that there is a life cycle in mentoring relationships; move it to the next phase, or bring it to a natural conclusion

- Keep a record of how you have benefited from mutual mentoring conversations so that you consistently apply that learning

44 WORK-SHADOW TEAM LEADERS IN OTHER SPHERES

WORK-SHADOWING A LEADER of a team in another sphere will give insights about how they prioritise, motivate and ensure effective outcomes. You will be surprised how much is transferable.

The idea

Work-shadowing involves thinking hard about the context you are observing and the dynamics of the team. You have to be observing both what is said and what is unsaid. Work-shadowing involves understanding the emotions of the participants, the dynamics in the room and how conclusions are reached.

Work-shadowing leaders in other spheres gives you a perspective about how they handle very different types of issues whilst working within similar constraints to you in terms of time, resources, histories and expectations.

As you work-shadow other team leaders, it is helpful to have some key questions in mind to use as a framework, for example, 'How does this leader build engagement and apply that engagement to reach outcomes which relevant parties are willing to accept?' When you work-shadow another leader, ensure there is enough time at the end to seek an understanding of why they took the decisions they did so you can interrelate your first reactions to their more considered perspective.

Saddique work-shadowed the leader of a firm of solicitors that was similar in size to his architectural practice. The work-shadowing included sitting in on a meeting of the leadership team and on some smaller meetings. This gave Saddique a valuable set of insights about leading a group of professionals who had a different approach from the architects. He observed how the leader of the solicitor's firm used his time, balancing it between building the business, managing the people, and doing his own professional work.

Saddique also work-shadowed the leader of a team of social workers in a local authority. He wanted to understand the dynamics within a public sector organisation and the way the team leader operated with a very different group of professional staff. In both these cases, there was valuable learning about how to widen the horizons of professional staff and ensure they were not too focused on their own narrow interests.

In practice

- Be willing to set aside time to work-shadow team leaders in other spheres

- Deliberately choose people in either similar or contrasting spheres and be clear what is the type of learning you want from the work-shadowing

- Before work-shadowing an individual, seek to understand the underlying issues and then be observant about what is said and what is unsaid

- Always be generous in your feedback to those people who have committed time to let you work-shadow them

- Respect – absolutely – the confidentiality of work-shadowing opportunities

- Be willing to give constructive feedback to those people you work-shadow if they are receptive to this

45 | TAKE A STEP CHANGE IN YOUR CONFIDENCE

Recognising the progress you have made as a team leader enables you to make a step change in your confidence and boldness.

The idea

Confidence and effectiveness often grow in steps rather than in a straight line. It can be immensely valuable to take stock and reflect on the progress you have made in leading a team, and then to consider how to build on this progress and become a more confident and effective team leader. Looking back can help remind you of how you tackled difficult situations and made a constructive impact. A stock-take allows you to affirm that ability and confidence in yourself and then to move into a new situation with the knowledge that you have been through demanding situations before and come out of them with good experience and a greater confidence.

Self-belief is not about arrogance; it is recognising that you have gifts and experience that have been tried and tested. Self-belief brings the confidence that you can tackle new and demanding issues based on a track record of success and adaptability.

Component elements of a step change in confidence include reflecting on what matters to you most, reframing what you think is possible going forward, rebalancing the relationship between the professional and the personal, and renewing your focus on what is possible through bringing a lightness of touch.

I often ask people, 'What would you do in this situation if you were bold?' When they have responded I then ask them, 'What is stopping you from doing this?' Asking yourself these two questions can help crystallise what you would do if you were more confident.

Saddique asked himself, 'What would I do if I were bolder?' His response was that he wanted to get the team of architects to face up to reality more sharply, and to be more explicit about the need for change. He would be more demanding of his architects about expecting them to think through how they were going to adapt to a changing environment and bring a greater focus on winning business. This was not about Saddique directing the architects on what to do, but about creating an expectation and conversations where the architects were more demanding of each other and clearer about the progress they wanted to make.

In practice

- Recognise the step changes that have taken place during your career

- Take stock of the progress you have made in recent months and how far you have stepped up in that time

- Reflect on the reality of your current situation and the changing expectations upon you

- Be bold in thinking through what is the step change you need to make and how to ensure you make that step change

- Imagine the step change you want to make and visualise it before you take it

- Remember that progress comes through taking a sequence of steps forward

46 KEEP DEVELOPING YOUR APPROACH TO COMMUNICATION

ADAPTING YOUR APPROACH to communication in the light of changing contexts and team membership is vital.

The idea

Good communication is the lifeblood of any team and organisation. Communication needs to be fresh and engaging, with a variety of approaches that take account of the changing context and the preferences of individuals. With the growth of social media and the increasing sophistication of information technology, the means of communication are continually evolving.

In rapidly changing contexts, communication needs to be fast and focused. At other times, communication can be more reflective, with opportunities for a wider range of people to contribute.

What works well varies between teams. Some teams get used to quick-fire e-mail exchanges. For other teams, stand-up meetings provide the best way of exchanging information quickly. Texting has resulted in much greater use of short, focused messages.

What is important is to have a combination of approaches to communication that meet the needs of individuals and provide for different types of engagement. Sometimes communication is just about information sharing. Sometimes it is setting a context in which decisions can be made more effectively. On other occasions it is creating a space for dialogue where the outcome is anticipated to be different from where the conversation began.

Effective team leaders repeat their messages again and again. They may get bored with their messages, but on each occasion it may be different people hearing the message. People may need to hear a message a few times before they begin to believe it. Consistency of message needs to be combined with adaptability of approach and the use of a range of different mediums.

Saddique had relied upon regular, structured meetings with his team of architects. He decided he needed to vary his approach with them and began to have more one-to-one conversations to identify issues of particular concern to individual architects. He decided to have a couple of more reflective half-day conversations in another location, where he encouraged the architects to open up about their hopes and aspirations.

Saddique held an open forum with all the staff at the practice where he talked through recent results and plans for the next year. Saddique deliberately used a more engaged and open style: he differentiated between when he was giving firm steers and when he was encouraging open debate. Saddique tried to bring more of a freshness to these conversations and encouraged this approach to be cascaded throughout the whole organisation.

In practice

- Be deliberate about the range of communication approaches you use

- Vary the style of communication using a mix of written and oral approaches

- Do not rely on one formula: recognise that different meetings have different purposes and require different approaches

- Make use of social media to draw out the views of different groups of staff

47 WIDEN YOUR REPERTOIRE OF APPROACHES, INCLUDING ROLE-PLAYING HOW YOU MIGHT LEAD DIFFERENTLY

WIDENING THE ARRAY of approaches you use as a leader, including role-playing how you might lead differently, can give you greater confidence in your adaptability as a leader.

The idea

The best of leaders can vary their approach with ease depending on the context. They can do command and control in a crisis; they can be consultative when there is open negotiation. They can be enabling when they have good direct reports capable of taking on demanding roles effectively.

Whenever you observe a team leader, ask yourself, 'What am I going to adopt in my approach drawn from this individual?' It can be useful to role-play other individuals. In any negotiation between teams, it can be helpful to sit in the seat of someone you are negotiating with in order to understand their perspective and to be able to argue their points.

If an individual is finding it difficult to understand another person, or is engaged in a dispute, I often suggest that they take on the mantle and approach of the other individual so that they fully understand what matters to that person and how that person interprets current reality and opportunities.

I have often suggested to people that they should try thinking and acting as if they are at a level higher than their current level in an organisation. The more they begin to think and act at a higher level, the more confidence they begin to display and the more likely it is that other people will treat them as someone at this higher level.

Saddique wanted to focus his leadership at a more strategic level. He decided to imagine how he would lead on longer-term issues in the community charity. He began to rehearse how he was going to handle a forthcoming senior team meeting in the architectural practice. Saddique found it helpful to practise in front of a mirror. As he observed himself, he was also listening to his words. This helped him be more confident about his understanding of opportunities going forward, and about how best the team could respond to the changing context.

Saddique encouraged the use of role-play within the architectural practice, with some of the architects playing the part of the clients. This helped the architects get into the minds and hearts of their clients. The result was a realisation for the architects that they needed to present their ideas in a more engaged and sensitive way.

In practice

- Always seek to expand your repertoire of approaches

- Try out different approaches in different contexts to develop your learning

- Encourage the use of role-play within your team to help people understand where others are coming from

- Encourage your team to act at a level up to help build their confidence and perspective, and to ensure that they do not get bogged down in detail

48 BUILD YOUR SUCCESSION AND ENSURE YOU ARE DISPENSABLE

You are building momentum for the future, hence the importance of ensuring succession and recognising that you are dispensable.

The idea

Every team leader has a responsibility to build succession both for their role and other key roles in the team. This is not an optional activity. If you are building momentum for a team, your credibility depends on a realism about succession.

This is rarely about creating a 'crown prince'. It is more often about cultivating two or three people within the organisation who have the skills, experience and confidence to be able to move into the team leader role. Or it might be about developing your role in such a way that there are candidates from other parts of the organisation or outside who would be equipped and confident enough to do your job – perhaps even better than you.

Developing people who could take over your leadership role means active investment in them. You need to give them the opportunity to build an understanding about the full range of activities you are dealing with and to develop their confidence in leading on cross-cutting issues. A message to those who are your potential successors might be the importance of acting collaboratively and adaptively so that they are equipped for a range of different leadership roles and not just the one you currently occupy.

Some would say that seeking to make yourself dispensable is a high-risk strategy. However, the duty of a team leader is to create an organisation that would continue to be effective even if the current leader was taken out of the equation. If you create a situation where you are indispensable, it can often end with the organisation falling apart after you leave.

If you are able to take a long holiday or a sabbatical, this can be a good moment to ensure that your leadership team takes on the full range of your responsibilities. Then you can observe how they rise to the occasion and what they are able to deliver on your return.

Saddique recognised that his job included a wider range of leadership and management functions than did the roles of his team leaders. He recognised that he needed to build up the confidence and capability of some of his team leaders so that they could take on wider leader responsibilities and be his potential successors.

Saddique took informal soundings amongst the team to see who would be interested in taking on some more management responsibilities, and talked about his ideas in the wider leadership team of architects. Most of them preferred that others took on the leadership co-ordination responsibilities. He gave cross-cutting responsibilities to two of the architects who were positive about taking on management responsibilities and sent them on a one-week leadership development programme. He began to consult them about decisions and encouraged them to become more confident in the way he took forward cross-cutting projects.

In practice

- Make it one of your objectives to work yourself out of the job
- Invest time in developing people who can succeed you

- Recognise the range of competences that people need in order to move up to a bigger management role and ensure that people with potential get those opportunities

- See every job as a stepping stone to some other activity so you do not become too reliant on the self-esteem you receive from doing this particular role

- When someone says to you that your job is completed, view that as a positive mark of respect and not purely a hint that it is time to move on

- Be objective about when is it in the best interests of the organisation for you to move on

49 TRUST YOUR INTUITIVE JUDGEMENT MORE

OUR INTUITIVE JUDGEMENT is an amalgam of all our values and experiences; it is rarely random.

The idea

There will always be reasons why we are reacting in a particular way even though they are not obvious. Sometimes our intuitive judgement is misguided and dominated by emotional considerations. Our intuitive judgements need to triangulated with trusted others.

I often ask leaders who are wrestling with different priorities, 'What is it that only you can do?' Their immediate response provides a good insight into where they should be spending their time. Sometimes as a leader you get bogged down and feel boxed in when ideally you need to be able to stand back and ask yourself, 'What is my gut telling me that I need to focus on?'

This approach then leads to questions like 'What are the opportunities that only I can unlock and take forward?' or 'What are the key risks I need to take responsibility for addressing?' It is not about taking a lot of burdens on your shoulders; the intent is to use these questions to decide on your top priorities and then ensure that other things are taken forward by other people or not done at all.

I led a workshop recently with a senior team looking at priorities in a range of different areas. For this meeting there were no papers, just an agenda. The intent was to use quick-fire small-group discussions to surface key opportunities and problems. Splitting the team into small groups meant that everyone had the opportunity to articulate their concerns and respond to the views of others.

The resulting product was not a detailed analysis and did not pretend to be such. It was a valuable list of intuitive concerns and opportunities which then needed to be examined and taken forward in more detail.

Saddique was conscious that the team seemed blind to opportunities in the retail sector. Their previous concentration had been within the public sector and financial institutions. Some of the architects felt the retail world was cheap and shoddy. Saddique trusted his instinct and explored what might be opportunities within the retail sector. He got a couple of the younger architects engaged in thinking through opportunities. Together they presented a plan to the wider group of architects, who began to see that there might be more opportunities there than they had previously thought.

Saddique got each of his senior team members to do a five-minute presentation about future opportunities. They were each asked to pick out two ideas and use an illustration to describe for each idea what might be possible. Each of them brought two creative architectural drawings and talked enthusiastically about opportunities they wanted to explore.

In practice

- See your intuitive judgement as the amalgam of your wisdom and experience

- Create situations where people need to give their immediate reactions and observe the pattern of reactions from different team members

- Create a balance between creative 'top of the head' thinking and 'bottom up' analysis

- Allow your intuitive judgement to be a good first indicator of key questions and priorities

BUILD IN FEEDBACK LOOPS

GOOD-QUALITY FEEDBACK is the most valuable gift you can be given.

The idea

Feedback that is all praise or all criticism has limited value. Feedback that differentiates between what has worked well or less well and gives indicators about potential progress going forward is hugely useful.

It can be worth inviting team members to observe a particular aspect of the way you are leading and to comment on that dimension. Your giving a steer about what you want them to observe in you will mean that your colleagues will be able to give you more focused feedback.

If you have been working on a particular aspect of the way you lead a team, invite team members to comment on whether they have seen any change in your approach. You may or may not want to 'lead the witness' by pointing out areas where you hope they might have observed changes.

It can be valuable to have a feedback loop with other parts of the organisation that you and your team are seeking to influence. Open-ended questions like 'What do you observe about the way we are seeking to build commitment and energy going forward?' can reveal what is working well or less well. Asking 'What are the outcomes or behaviour changes that we as a team need to focus on?' can reveal a set of priorities that is different from inherited expectations.

Saddique felt there was a feedback vacuum. He did not know whether his leadership approach was appreciated by either his architects or the firm's clients. The open-ended question 'What might I do differently?' did not produce a very helpful response when he put it directly to individuals in the team.

Saddique asked the team coach to seek feedback from different team members about what was working well and less well in the leadership he brought. The team coach pressed people gently but firmly for explanations of their initial thoughts. In this way the team coach built up a clear picture about what aspects of Saddique's leadership approach were producing a positive approach and what aspects he might need to look at again.

Saddique arranged for a structured sequence of interviews with key clients about the work of the organisation, including the part he played. The results tied in with his perception of a reliable, if sometimes a little unadventurous, group of architects. The absence of much comment about his leadership was a wakeup call that he needed to think carefully about what should be his relationship, as practice leader, with client organisations.

In practice

- Have an appetite for feedback but treat it with care
- Be specific about the areas where you would like feedback and then ensure you take the feedback seriously
- Seek to have a range of different feedback loops both within and outside the organisation so that you can find patterns
- See critical feedback as just as useful as positive feedback
- Never be afraid of feedback: it is an invaluable contribution to your continued development

SECTION F
ENSURING EFFECTIVE TEAMS ACROSS YOUR ORGANISATION

51. SET A CONSTRUCTIVE EXAMPLE

THE WAY YOU ORGANISE your team cascades through other teams within your part of the organisation, hence the importance of setting a constructive example.

The idea

The example you set as a team will be followed whether you like it or not. Members of your team may well default to organising their team in the same way as you lead your team. They will build in their own variations, but their starting position may well be to follow the pattern you set.

Other people in the organisation who observe your team may mirror some of its features without deliberately intending to do so. They will assume, either explicitly or implicitly, that this is the way of 'doing things around here'. If other people in the organisation perceive your team as not working well, their instinctive reaction will be to lead their teams in a different way, so that they are not seen as being associated with your team.

Setting a constructive example will mean explaining what you do and why you do it. You may be assuming that your way of leading a team is the right one and not explain your reasons. But the clearer you are in explaining your approach and rationale, the more readily people will follow you, and the easier it is for others to recognise why you are leading the team in the way you are.

Part of setting a constructive example is to adapt the way you and your team do things in the light of changing circumstances and then to explain clearly why you have made the changes. The more you can give a clear account of how and why you have responded to changing circumstances the better.

Mary was a manager of a big retail store and had senior team members working for her who were running different departments. She held regular meetings with her senior team. Some of the meetings were brisk and focused on the week ahead, while others were more reflective, looking at different priorities. Mary instituted a cascade system to keep members of staff up to speed on the day-to-day business, and engaged separately with them on longer-term issues.

Mary recognised that whatever pattern she established would be mirrored by the departmental managers, hence she was meticulous in talking with team members individually and collectively about how they were going to work together and how best they would listen to each other and challenge each other. Mary kept her regular pattern of discussions in place for six months to ensure it was coherent and understood. Only then did she make some changes, which she explained with care because she knew that confusion was never far below the surface.

In practice

- Recognise that the example you set will be the default approach for your team members with their teams

- Always set aside enough time to explain what you are doing and why

- Embed values that are important to you in the way you interact with your team

- Maintain consistency in your approach so that team members recognise the pattern of interaction and are able to apply it in the teams they lead

52 SHARE EXAMPLES OF GOOD PRACTICE

THE MORE EXAMPLES of good practice that are shared the better, so that team members are curious about what is working well and adaptable enough to build on best practice.

The idea

When a team gets into a rhythm of working that seems productive and enjoyable, there is a risk that it starts to close in on itself and think that this way of working is optimal. Team leaders will of course want their team members to feel positive about being part of the team and believe that they are making progress. But the forward-looking team leader will also want members of the team to be curious about how other teams are working.

In a team that is working well, the members will be proud of what they are doing and continually seeking out examples of good practice. Most team members are likely to be involved in a range of different teams both inside work and outside.

A helpful conversation can be prompted by team leaders sharing their experience of working in teams outside the immediate team and encouraging other team members to do the same. Valuable insights can be gained by talking through examples of good practice with people who are members of teams in a voluntary capacity within their community or in a sport.

There will almost inevitably be parallels that can be drawn and illustrations of how team members have been motivated and been creative in using their different skills and interests. Sharing examples reminds team members that there is always more than one way of working together.

Mary often drew examples from teams she had been a member of before. She would refer to leadership teams she had been part of in other parts of the company as well as outside the organisation, drawing out their strengths and limitations.

Mary invited members of the team to do the same. She created an atmosphere where people could be open in commenting on best practice within the current team. She was not defensive if people said they had observed other teams working more effectively in some aspects. She always demonstrated an appetite to learn from whatever examples of good practice her team members were willing to share.

In practice

- Be open to sharing examples of good practice from your past experience, and invite others to do the same

- Be willing to share examples that illustrate both success and failure, and draw out the lessons learnt

- Demonstrate in both your words and your demeanour that you are open to learning and building in good practice from elsewhere

- Take time to write up examples of good practice that you think are worth sharing so that you can draw from them on future occasions

53 MAINTAIN A REGULAR DIALOGUE ABOUT WHAT MAKES AN EFFECTIVE TEAM

IT IS WORTH DEVELOPING an openness to sharing experiences about what is working well or less well as a team and how that experience can be built upon.

The idea

Members of your organisation are likely to be part of a variety of different teams. You want to engender an atmosphere of continuous learning so people are reflecting on what has worked well or less well in the teams they are part of.

Within your own team, you want to set an example of open dialogue. If you can generate this openness in your team, it prompts others to adopt a similar practice so that review and continuous learning become a standard part of the way the organisation operates.

Ensuring regular dialogue about what makes an effective team is not intended to be perpetually inward-looking self-examination. What you are seeking to promote is constructive, thoughtful and focused discussion. This can be done through inviting team members to suggest, briefly, one approach that the team has used recently that could be built on further. Or you could prompt a conversation inviting team members to share a piece of learning from their involvement in another team that is transferable. The more you encourage short, focused, 'in the moment' discussions about effective teams, the quicker and more responsive the learning will be.

As you work with individual team members about their future development, it can be helpful to prompt them to have regular conversations with their peers about what makes an effective team. The more peers are able to share pertinent examples, the quicker the learning and application of the learning are likely to be.

Mary often took time at the end of a meeting to ask team members to share one example of where the team was working well. She would often follow this by asking what was one thing the team ought to be doing differently. Sometimes she would prompt such a discussion whilst a team was seated around a table. On other occasions she deliberately prompted this type of discussion when the team members had stood up at the end of a meeting. Mary wanted to create contexts where people would respond briefly and honestly. She encouraged one-liners, which often revealed someone's emotional reactions more openly than a considered response.

In practice

- Prompt short discussions about what has worked well or less well

- Use occasions when people are standing up to elicit one-line reactions and then prompt some brief, follow-up conversation

- Be specific in your questions so that discussion is focused

- Use open questions, which do not imply a preferred answer, to prompt honest reactions

- Remember that a lot of progress can be made in a five-minute conversation if you are prompting open and quick interaction

- Respect people's preferences and distinguish between those people with whom you can have a quick-fire dialogue and those who need more reflection time

54 ENCOURAGE PARTNERSHIPS BETWEEN DIFFERENT PARTS OF THE ORGANISATION

WHERE THERE IS an effective partnership, there will be a greater openness to learning and a greater willingness to share experience.

The idea

Partnerships can have very different characteristics. Some are formal, with a written contract of engagement. Others are informal, and will be about mutual sharing and learning.

There may need to be a formal contract of engagement between, say, the Information Technology team and the Operations Director. The team leader who is able to draw out the best in the respective teams will see the partnership as much more than a contract. A good partnership is about shared endeavour based around a common purpose. A formal partnership between two teams works best when there is a shared understanding about the outcomes that are sought and an appreciation of the contributions that the two teams are going to make.

When two teams are working well in partnership, there is openness and transparency about progress and frustrations; the teams recognise how best to support each other and bring out the best in each other.

A good informal partnership will always have a sense of shared enterprise and an emotional engagement that makes people want to spend time with each other. Developing a sense of fun is just as important as any written contract.

Mary was conscious that her senior team at her big store needed to work with a key team at the distribution centre. She ensured that the two teams had the opportunity to meet even though they worked in different locations. She worked hard to ensure there was a good informal understanding between them.

The teams had to operate within clear operational guidelines and have their performance assessed. But this did not stop them developing an understanding of the pressures the other team faced and how best they could mutually support each other. The two teams recognised that they depended on each other's expertise and commitment. Because they got to know each other, they developed a sense of mutual responsibility and a willingness to support each other and modify some of their requests when the other team was under immediate pressure because of the absence of key staff.

In practice

- Use the language of partnership to describe the links between different teams

- Be willing to invest time in building up the quality of a partnership

- Seek to find and articulate the common purpose that brings together different teams

- Recognise that the nature of the partnership between different teams is influenced by how formal the contract needs to be

- Recognise that what makes a partnership successful is a combination of shared purpose and a good level of mutual support and understanding

55. ENCOURAGE PARTICIPATION IN A RANGE OF DIFFERENT TEAMS

PEOPLE WHO ARE involved in multiple teams experience different ways of working and different leadership styles, which helps to widen their experience and understanding.

The idea

As a team leader, you want members to be committed to the team and its objectives. But you do not want team members who are so blinkered that they do not see why others view this enterprise differently. You want your team members to bring a range of experiences and understanding so that they contribute to the team in a committed, objective and adaptable way.

If it sometimes feels that your team is being opposed by central or corporate teams, it can be valuable to arrange for one of your team members to be part of a central or corporate team. This experience will give them a wider understanding of why people react as they do and why decisions are made in a particular way in the centre. This individual can then act as an interpreter to help build understanding of why people in different parts of the organisation approach issues in different ways.

Mary was conscious that her departmental heads were very committed to the success of the retail store. However, there were lots of complaints about the central departments in Head Office and suggestions that those working at the centre did not understand what it was like working in a big store.

The Director of Operations was setting up a number of cross-cutting teams to look at various new initiatives as well as training and development practices. Mary thought that this was a great opportunity to give wider experience to some of her senior people. Two of them became involved in these cross-cutting groups. The deal with these two individuals was that they would come back with insights from elsewhere in the organisation about how different teams operated. Mary asked these two people to contribute from these experiences to prompt discussion in her leadership team about best practice. This always led to lively discussions.

The experience of these two team members was especially helpful in bringing an understanding of the background to certain central decisions and an insight into how best to influence decisions being made in the centre. Mary ensured that all the members of the team saw the benefit of the wider experience that the two people had gained. The result was that each member of her team wanted to take part in a central initiative. This enhanced the effectiveness and reputation of Mary's whole team.

In practice

- Ensure team members have some available time that they can use to contribute to other teams

- Be explicit with them about the type of learning you want them to gain from this experience

- Create opportunities for the sharing of learning from their participation in wider teams

- Enable feedback from an individual's participation in a different team to be reflected in his or her overall performance review

56 | ENCOURAGE THE SHADOWING OF OTHER TEAMS

WORK-SHADOWING ANOTHER TEAM can lead to new insights about best practice.

The idea

When a leader is work-shadowed, it forces the leader to think about their actions and articulate why they are doing what they are doing. The person who is doing the shadowing sees someone leading in real time and is able to ask pertinent questions. A reflective conversation at the end of a day of work-shadowing provides insights for both people.

The same benefits can be reaped from observing and shadowing a team. The astute Chair will invite someone who has been work-shadowing his team to share their perceptions after a team meeting. On the first occasion, the team leader might do this privately. But the main benefit comes from having the whole team hear the feedback.

If a member of your team is going to work-shadow another team, it is worth discussing what that person is going to be looking for. You want this person to do this without a preconceived view about what is good practice, to observe the dynamics and processes with an open mind, and then to reflect on three or four points of learning that could be fed back into their current team.

Mary observed that one of her team leaders, Bill, was less adaptable than she would have liked, and his contributions to the team seemed defensive. Bill did not always appear as if he was listening in order to learn; he seemed to be listening in order to refute. Bill's commitment was clear, but there was a slowness to learn. Mary agreed with Bill that work-shadowing a leadership team in another big store would give him a wider perspective. Bill was initially reluctant but accepted that it would be worth a try.

The experience radically changed Bill's perspective. He quickly recognised the dynamics in this different team. He observed someone in the team who was defensive and saw how this had a negative effect on others. Bill was shocked to observe someone who was rather like himself and the adverse effect of this person's interventions. The consequence was that Bill shifted the way he contributed, which led to much more open interaction with his current team members.

In practice

- See work-shadowing as mutually beneficial to both parties
- Be focused in shaping expectations about the learning that can come through work-shadowing
- See work-shadowing as a time-effective way of leadership development
- Encourage an individual who work-shadows another team to feed back their learning to their current team
- Build mutual work-shadowing work arrangements between members of parallel teams to maximise the learning

57 · REWARD AND RECOGNISE EFFECTIVE TEAMS

TEAMS THAT ARE RECOGNISED and rewarded will feel that their behaviour and personal investment have been worthwhile. As a consequence they will be more likely to repeat that behaviour.

The idea

William Haig, who was the British Foreign Secretary from 2010 to 2014, won the respect and affection of staff in the Foreign Office because he was consistent in recognising the contribution that staff right across the organisation were making. The staff had a tough job with limited resources, but Haig's clarity of priorities and his consistent, overt recognition of staff contributions meant that commitment levels were always high.

The more you recognise the contribution of individuals and teams, the greater will be the level of self-belief and commitment. Blanket praise like 'You have done well' is not as effective as praise that is focused on activities and behaviours that work well. The most powerful way in which a team improves is through positive reinforcement.

In some organisations, financial reward is regarded as the only worthwhile incentive. But this is a very one-dimensional way of thinking. Reward could also be a team celebration, or the whole team leaving work early on a Friday afternoon, or a shared decision to raise money for a charitable cause. A reward of a good dinner could be part of an away day when most of the time is spent in reflective deliberation on good practice and learning going forward.

Mary was disciplined in drawing out what the team had been doing well. She was careful to give recognition to the contribution that team members had made to the overall work of the team. She would describe her observations about how individual team members had enabled other members of the team to be at their best.

Mary recognised that she needed to reward individual members of the team financially as part of the organisation's pay arrangements. There was also the flexibility to provide modest team bonuses which she used in a focused way, always making sure to explain why a team bonus had been given.

In practice

- Spend time articulating the effectiveness you observe in your team

- Bring out the contribution of team members in enabling other team members to be effective

- Sing the praises of your team's effectiveness both internally within the team and externally across the organisation

- Reflect on what different types of reward you can use

- Seek to minimise the divisive effect of financial rewards by giving clear reasons for decisions

- If you are able to apply team bonuses, do it in a way that reinforces the right approaches and behaviours

58. ENSURE THAT DIVERSITY IS RECOGNISED

Acknowledging the benefits of diversity helps to reinforce those benefits, so that diversity is seen as a strength and not as a problem.

The idea

The image of the successful team as a group of wise, elderly men in suits is thankfully long gone. The best of teams include a mixture of people of different genders, ages and cultural perspectives. A group of individuals with different social, financial, ethnic and geographic backgrounds can bring a wealth of experience and insight, as well as a variety of ways of addressing complex issues.

The benefits that come from having a diverse team are worth highlighting, but the words have to be carefully chosen to avoid embarrassment or stereotyping. Gentle humour about the creativity of youth and the wisdom of age can be helpful in ensuring that every participant feels valued. Recognising diversity also includes making allowance for the circumstances or commitments of individuals, be they family commitments or religious practices.

Mary saw the diversity in her team as a strength. Amar was relatively quiet but always insightful. By background he was an Indian Hindu. Mary was sensitive to his background and faith and saw his approach as a valuable part of the team.

At an away day she invited the members of the team to talk about an aspect of their cultural or religious background that was important to them and how that influenced the way they contributed to the team. Amar was very thoughtful in talking about gentleness and finding a shared endeavour. The rest of the team understood more now about why Amar might contribute in the way that he did. This openness led to lots of positive affirmation about the way Amar contributed going forward so that his contribution was even more influential.

In practice

- See diversity as a strength and not a weakness

- Accept that where there is diversity it may take longer for team members to understand and appreciate each other

- Recognise how having a diverse team enhances the quality of dialogue and output

- Create contexts where people can talk about how their cultural and religious background and beliefs influence the way they contribute to the team

- Demonstrate to the wider organisation the strengths that come from having a diverse team

- Recognise the continued investment of time that will be needed to ensure the quality of dialogue between people of very different backgrounds and perspectives

59 ENABLE TEAMS TO END WELL

ENDINGS ARE AS IMPORTANT as beginnings. They ensure a crystallisation of learning and a sound foundation for the future.

The idea

A lot of effort goes into starting a new team and building a clear prospectus and strong relationships, but when a team completes its work there can be a drifting off and an anti-climax.

Enabling a team to end well includes a crystallisation of learning so people move on feeling positive about what the team has achieved. Individual differences need to be taken into account. For some people, when a team has completed its work, their desire is to get on with the next task. Others need a period of reflection – or even grieving – before they are ready to move on.

When a team has completed a project or task, as team leader you have a golden opportunity to celebrate the output, ensure good-quality recognition across the organisation and help people to crystallise their learning and move on in a positive frame of mind.

When external factors mean an organisation has to be restructured, or senior management decides that current arrangements have not worked effectively and a new team structure needs to be put in place, any sense of celebration seems inappropriate. But the need for a team to end well is just as important. There will always be things to mark, even if the outcomes are relatively disappointing.

There will always have been some areas of progress or some types of interaction and analysis that have gone well. There will always have been learning by team members. As team leader, you may want to move on quickly, but investing some time in sharing the grief or disappointment and identifying the learning is never wasted. What you are doing is enabling people to build a foundation for the future, irrespective of whether the outcome of the current team's work appears to be a magnificent edifice or a pile of rubble.

Mary was conscious that her leadership team was going to lose two members. She thought it important to mark the ending of this phase of the work of the team. The departure of these two members tied in well with the delivery of some changes in the store and the achievement of some sales targets.

Mary marked their departure by recognising what they, individually, had done and what the team as a whole had delivered over recent months. She deliberately portrayed the work of the team as reaching a good ending so the departing people left on a positive note. Her approach was designed to ensure that there was a new start with new team members for the next phase of the work.

In practice

- See good-quality endings as just as important as good beginnings

- Recognise the different needs of people in the way endings are marked

- Accept that for some people endings are not important – their desire is to move on as quickly as possible

- Accept that some people will go through a period of grief as a team concludes its work

- Always draw out the learning from endings and celebrate what was distinctive about what the team delivered well

60 BUILD IN EFFECTIVE LEARNING WHEN TEAMS ARE DISBANDED

THE QUESTION OF 'What is the learning you take from this experience?' when a team comes to an end is always worth asking.

The idea

When a team is disbanded, the emotional reactions range from anger, frustration, resentment and disappointment to grief. As team leader, you are likely to be sharing the same emotions. Your team members will be watching you. If you act as a robot, they will either disbelieve you or ignore you, but you will want to be selective about how you show your emotions.

You will need your own mechanism outside the team to talk through your emotional reactions, crystallise your learning and move on. You need to do that in parallel with your work with the team so that you can be deliberative in what you share with the team.

Try to be one step ahead of your team in terms of understanding your emotions, working with them and moving on. You may well want to share an element of your pain, while always putting it in the context of moving on in as positive a frame of mind as possible. Where the disbanding of a team can lead to new opportunities, it is worth highlighting what those opportunities might be for members of the team. Where the disbanding of a team is leading to uncertainty and potential redundancy, bringing honesty and openness to the inevitability of difficult outcomes will be appreciated – in the long term if not in the short term.

Best practice is about not hiding the truth, but putting it sensitively, situating it in a wider context, and looking for possibilities going forward. Part of the positive message is about the learning gained and how that can be put to good use. A constant refrain of 'There is always learning that is transferable' is a valuable reminder.

Mary was initially heartbroken when she heard that two stores were going to be combined under one leadership team. This meant the disbanding of her team. She chose the moment carefully to tell her team. Her words were of thanks to them for their contribution and a drawing out of the reasons for the changes and the opportunities for the two stores that this change would create. Mary recognised that some team members were able to see the benefits and the opportunities, while others initially only saw downsides and the potential dilution of their work.

Mary's task was to bring realism about how best to handle whatever was going to happen going forward. She was patient and clear with her team leaders, recognising that each of them was on a journey getting used to this change. Her constant refrain was, 'What is the learning from this team that you can take forward into future teams you are part of?'

In practice

- Be as prepared as you can for how you would respond to a situation where your team is being disbanded

- Know who you would talk to outside the team to work through your emotions and next steps

- Bring openness, honesty and a sense of realism to discussions about the future

- Enable people to recognise that any ending, however painful, builds resilience going forward

SECTION G
BEING AN AUTHORITATIVE TEAM MEMBER

61 KNOW WHAT THE LEADER WANTS AND WHERE YOU CAN CONTRIBUTE

EFFECTIVE TEAM MEMBERS need to understand what the leader wants and where they can contribute.

The idea

When you are asked to be part of a team, there may be a range of areas where you would like to contribute. You may feel a sense of excitement about what you can offer or how the team should go in a different direction. You may believe you bring lots of wisdom to the team that they would be foolish to ignore.

The right starting point is to ask why you have been appointed and what are the expectations about your contribution from those who appointed you. If you were appointed because you bring particular expertise or a perspective from a particular group, it is important to recognise that. Your initial credibility may well depend on your responding to those expectations.

It is worth having an open discussion with the leader about what they want and where you can contribute. Although it may be for a particular reason that you were invited, it is perfectly reasonable to talk about how else you might contribute. You can then get a sense of how such a contribution would be received. You may only agree to be a member of the team if there is enough scope for you to contribute in a supplementary area or in a way that is important to you. Or, there may be areas where you would like to contribute which are not current priorities for the team. You may still decide to become a member, with your contribution likely to evolve over time.

It is worth checking with the team leader periodically whether your contribution continues to be what is needed and to explore in such stock-take conversations how you might develop the contribution you make to the team.

Rashid was asked to be part of a team developing training modules in an international organisation. She felt honoured to be asked but posed direct questions to the team leader about why she had been approached. She wanted to ensure it was not just because she widened the racial, age and gender balance.

When Rashid was satisfied that she was being invited to be a member of this team for good reasons, she explored with the team leader the areas in which she could take a particular interest. She said that she wanted to engage in developing effective training and development for emerging leaders who had family commitments. They reached an agreement that Rashid's annual performance assessment would include consideration of her contribution to this global work.

In practice

- Be willing to ask the team leader directly why you are being appointed
- Be clear in your own mind where you can contribute
- Recognise that your contribution will develop over time, hence the importance of building your credibility
- Be clear how you are going to meet the expectations of the team leader in the first few months so that there is positive reinforcement about the value of your appointment

62 RECOGNISE THE CONSTRAINTS UPON YOU

BEING AN EFFECTIVE TEAM member requires a recognition of the limitations of the scope of your contribution, the constraints upon you, and the impact you can have.

The idea

When you are appointed to a committee, it may seem a wonderful opportunity to change the organisation or its direction of travel. But there will be constraints: the committee or group may have clear terms of reference with no legitimacy outside this defined scope. Trying to persuade the team to do what it currently does not want to do is the fastest way to become sidelined and ignored. Sometimes the most effective results come from biding your time, building your credibility and choosing your moment to press for a new direction. Once people move on or the context changes, what was previously unthinkable might become possible.

Sometimes constraints come from your own time or role. In a busy job, and with wider personal commitments as well, the time available will be limited. It does not help your credibility to promise more than you are able to contribute. The constraints may mean that you agree early on how best you can contribute and how you want to measure that contribution with the team leader after a period of time.

Sometimes you may think the constraints upon you result from your lack of experience. In fact, your contribution could be all the more important because you do not know the detailed background. You bring fresh insights and the ability to ask key questions.

Rashid saw herself as one of the more junior and inexperienced members of the team. Initially she was inhibited, but over time she recognised that her constraints were self-imposed. The other members of the team welcomed her lively and fresh approach, and always engaged with her ideas. Rashid gradually was more demonstrative and more challenging in her contributions.

Rashid was pushing the boundaries in terms of how much she challenged the senior people in the organisation. Only once did she feel she overstepped the mark with a critical comment. Rashid was conscious that the time she could give to the committee was limited and she needed to prioritise where she offered to take work forward between meetings. This self-imposed constraint helped her work through where she could make the biggest difference and where she could work jointly with others.

In practice

- Be clear about the terms of reference and scope of a team so you understand what the formal constraints are

- Do due diligence by talking to others about what are the constraints working in the team

- Think through what are the self-imposed constraints you want to put on your own contribution because of time commitments

- Be mindful when you might be imposing constraints that are unnecessary limitations

- Be willing to push boundaries on constraints; observe to what extent there is push back from others

- If you think some constraints are unhelpful, seek an opportune moment to talk those constraints through with other colleagues and other team leaders

63 RECOGNISE HOW BEST TO BE INFLUENTIAL

THERE ARE MANY DIFFERENT WAYS to be influential; you need to adjust your approach to respond to the way the team works to get the best outcomes.

The idea

Influential team members employ a variety of different approaches to help shape the forward agenda. They use formal occasions to contribute clearly, and informal chats with colleagues to build trust and a sense of shared endeavour. They build alliances with other people within the organisation where there is a common interest, and keep in touch with people from outside the organisation whose views are important. They are constantly building a picture of the views of others with an interest in the success of this team, choosing the right moment to feed these perspectives into the deliberations of the team.

Being influential depends very much on timing – choosing the moment to make a point, ask a question, or invite someone to contribute who has a particularly pertinent viewpoint. Being influential does not mean talking at great length; it is about phrasing the question and putting it across with authority. It comes through engaging with others, building alliances, creating common cause and reinforcing the contributions of others.

Being influential is not about always getting your own way; it is about choosing those subjects which matter most to you and using your influence, authority and presence to shape the conversations and then outcomes in such areas. In any team you are part of, it is worth observing who is influential and reflecting on where their influence comes from – their experience, their networks, the perspectives they bring, or the questions they ask?

When you see how some people are influential in a team, you may be able to adopt some of the same approaches. It is helpful to ally yourself with influential people on some subjects so you receive some of their reflected authority. Talk to influential people in advance to see where they are coming from and ascertain whether they are likely to support the ideas you plan to put forward.

Rashid wanted to be influential in the group. She had lots of ideas to put forward but at the same time she recognised there was an interplay between existing members of the team. She needed to understand the dynamics and recognise whose opinions carried most weight. She began to have informal conversations with them prior to meetings to gain their perspective and share her views.

Rashid recognised that she would be listened to if her comments were positive, clear and relatively short. She understood the danger of over-preparing and having too detailed a speech ready. She soon realised that the shorter and more focused her interventions, the more influential they were likely to be. As soon as Rashid stopped 'trying too hard' and began to choose the moment to intervene, her contributions became more effective.

In practice

- Observe who is influential and how they exert their influence in the teams you are part of

- Understand the mix of formal and influencing approaches that work within a team and see how you can use both modes to good effect

- Build informal relationships with members of the team in

order to understand their perspective and how there can be mutual support

- Recognise who it might be difficult to influence and prepare your ground carefully if you want to shape their thinking

- Recognise the importance of timing

- Keep interventions short and focused

- See a good question as just as influential as a powerful statement

64 WATCH YOUR TONE OF VOICE AND BODY LANGUAGE

THE SIGNALS WE GIVE through our body language and tone of voice can be far more influential than the words we use.

The idea

How many meetings have you been to where someone's tone of voice or body language affected the whole meeting? If someone looks grumpy, their demeanour is noted and communicates itself across the room. Grumpiness in one person can soon become grumpiness in a whole meeting. On the other hand, if a key member of the group enters the room cheerful and engaging, this demeanour can rapidly have a positive effect on the others.

Part of becoming an influential member of a team is understanding how you come over to others. Does your tone of voice invite people to listen to you? Is there a rhythm in your voice that people respond to? Can you vary the pace in how you contribute to maintain people's interest? Can you engage people with your eyes and your shoulders so that they know you are aware of their presence?

If you look anxious and huddled in your own arms, you may become sidelined. When you sit forward with your arms open rather than closed, and your eyes engaged rather than looking down, you are much more likely to be listened to and influential.

If your shoulders drop and your voice becomes soft, it is the equivalent of opening a trapdoor and falling out of the room. Being domineering and aggressive is just as unproductive when it leads to other members of the team metaphorically turning their backs on you.

Rashid was nervous when she joined the global team. She tended to sit back and slightly slump in her chair. She then wondered why people ignored her. Once she got used to attending the meetings, she began to sit up and maintain eye contact with members of the group. Her furrowed brow gradually turned into a more open facial expression. Her natural smile showed more often. People looked at her and smiled back.

Rashid was conscious that sometimes the volume of her voice could drop. She practised keeping her voice firm prior to going into a meeting. She imagined herself in her family, where she often had to speak up to be heard. She trained herself to transmit her voice more strongly while ensuring that it did not become harsh.

Rashid built a trusting relationship with a couple of other members of the group and invited them to give her feedback about how she was coming over. This proved invaluable in forewarning her when she was becoming too quiet.

In practice

- Observe how others use their tone of voice and physical posture to good effect

- Be conscious when your voice drops or when you speak too quickly

- Ask a couple of trusted people in the teams you are part of to give you feedback about how you come over

- Sit with an open stance in meetings so you look engaged

- Remember that a smile is a powerful way of building allegiance with others

65 BE PREPARED TO CHALLENGE AN ESTABLISHED TEAM

ONE OF THE MOST valuable contributions a new team member can make is to be willing to challenge an established team's way of doing things, to keep it relevant and fresh.

The idea

Every team establishes a particular way of doing things that it is comfortable with. This may include the times at which meetings take place, the way people intervene, the order of contributions, or the timing of the coffee breaks. There may be a particular routine about who speaks first. There may be unwritten norms about behaviours and about the types of actions that are permissible.

Observing the interactions of a team will show you which of these routines are working well and which ones have outlived their usefulness. A team can become complacent without realising it.

Challenging an established team involves asking questions about why certain things are done in particular ways and why certain possibilities are not explored. Innocent questions can lead to thoughtful conversation. Sometimes an established team is best challenged through building alliances with individual members and getting them to think in slightly different ways. On other occasions, the most effective approach is to address an issue head on, and invite a review about why things are always done in a particular way or whether the factors considered should be broadened.

Rather than challenging a team directly, it can be a useful approach to ask whether it would be a good idea for the team to challenge itself about whether there might be a fresh way of tackling particular issues or whether a particular policy or decision needs to be reviewed.

It can be a necessary part of becoming accepted fully by a team to have challenged it in some way. What is then important is your demonstrating commitment to the success of the team so that other members do not feel you are sniping from the side. Once others see your commitment to the overall team's endeavour, they are more likely to respond thoughtfully to your challenges.

Rashid thought the global team was dated in its perspective. It put too much reliance on formal courses. She observed that her contemporaries gained far more from shorter workshops and focused learning sets. She recognised that she needed to speak up on this subject and challenge the accepted norms. She had collected good evidence about preferences and participation rates, and deployed this with care. She told the Chair that she was going to press this key point about the balance of priorities in the programme. As the Chair had been forewarned, she ensured a properly structured discussion of this subject.

In practice

- Do not be overawed by an established team

- Recognise that you have been appointed to that team and you have an equal right to voice your opinion as anyone else

- Be willing to speak your mind but choose your moment carefully and forewarn the team leader

- Be prepared to listen to others, while having facts and evidence ready to support your concerns

- When you challenge people, give them time to reflect and do not force an early decision unless it is absolutely essential

66 BRING REALITY AND A FRESH PERSPECTIVE TO AN UNCERTAIN TEAM

EVERY TEAM GOES THROUGH periods of uncertainty. Think about what contribution you can bring to help create renewed energy and a new way of looking at the future.

The idea

A team may reach a point where it is uncertain what to do next. This uncertainty may cause confusion, or there may be acceptance that some time needs to pass before clarity returns.

If you arrive as a new team member, the rest of the team may be embarrassed if there is uncertainty about next steps for the team. They will not want to be 'found out' by their newest member. Equally, they might be looking forward to your arrival, hoping you bring a different perspective. A risk is they will expect you to solve their problems straightaway. Whatever the case, the uncertainty provides a good opportunity to engage fully in finding a way forward.

As a new member, you may be able to see a reality that existing members have become blind to. Painting the reality as you see it – warts and all – is one of the most valuable contributions that you can make. Team members may have forgotten what they are good at and what they have done well in the past.

Your observations about strengths, weaknesses, threats and opportunities can be highly influential, providing a new frame of reference and enabling the team to think more positively about what they need to do and how to do it.

Rashid recognised that there was a dilemma that needed to be addressed about priorities for the development of staff with long-term potential. Various measures had been tried with limited success. Rashid had observed high-potential development programmes working effectively in a number of organisations. She recognised the mix of activities that needed to be included to ensure there was good-quality, personal learning in terms of self-awareness and understanding best practice across the globe.

When Rashid knew that a key discussion was about to happen in this global group, she did her research carefully and had firm evidence to share about what had worked well and less well. She put together some ideas about what would be possible and communicated those ideas with energy and commitment. There was a freshness in her voice, her language and her ideas. She caught the imagination of her colleagues, who agreed that a further discussion, with some high-potential staff, would be worthwhile. She had used the uncertainty in the team as an opening to put together a major new programme. There was relief in the group that a way forward had been found.

In practice

- See uncertainty in a team as an opportunity

- Build a clear understanding about the nature of that uncertainty and the level of willingness to find a way forward

- Paint reality as it is, backed up by hard evidence

- Be enthusiastic about any fresh perspective you bring and seek to build allies before the substantive discussion

- Be willing to bring others into the debate so that the decision does not rest solely on the eloquence of your words

67 DRAW OUT THE BEST IN OTHERS

DRAWING OUT THE BEST in others strengthens their contribution to the success of the team and allows you to contribute more effectively through the relationships and alliances you build.

The idea

When I work with teams, I invite people to say in plenary what they need from their colleagues to bring out the best in them. This often leads to surprising comments. I did this exercise recently with a team that was an equal mix of men and women. Broadly the women said they wanted more challenge from their colleagues to bring out the best in them, while the men said they needed more support and understanding from their colleagues. These reactions were entirely opposite to what the male/female stereotype might have expected. This was a revelation to the team. The resulting discussion was rich in building mutual understanding.

When I work with individual team members, I ask them who is committed to their success. I encourage them to build links with other members that are based on providing challenge and support, to enable each person to make the best contribution they can.

As you enter a new team, it will not take long before you have a picture of who you are most in tune with and who you need to tread more carefully with. You will soon develop an understanding of how you bring out the best in different members of the team by the way you contribute and the way you respond to their contributions.

Drawing out the best in others may seem self-limiting or vicarious, but the more you do so, the more you will be appreciated as an enabler and facilitator.

Rashid observed that a couple of other relatively new members of the global team were quiet and unassuming. She made a point of getting to know these two people. In discussions, she would deliberately look at them and draw in their contributions. Sometimes she would explicitly say in the group that these two individuals had an important contribution to make from their own experience.

Privately Rashid spoke with these two people about how they could bring out the best in each other and complement each other's approach. There was a mutual process of building confidence. They did not always take the same view, but they were willing to debate with each other about next steps.

Rashid suggested to the group that they ought to have a session as a team in which they explored the question of how they brought out the best in each other. This led to members working in pairs and threes on particular subjects. The group became ever more creative and engaging in its dialogue, because a mutual awareness had been built up as to how best each person could contribute.

In practice

- Recognise who brings out the best in you and how you bring out the best in others

- As you become established in a team, seek to bring out the best in others rather than seeking credit for yourself

- Celebrate with others when they have gone out of their comfort zone and demonstrated their effectiveness in areas where they had previously been hesitant

68 | SEE SUCCESS AS THE SUCCESS OF THE TEAM, NOT JUST YOUR PERSONAL SUCCESS

THE MORE YOU SEE success as the success of the team, the more authoritative you will become as a team member.

The idea

The most successful team I was part of was the senior management team of a Government department. There was a strong commitment to the success of the team rather than that of just the individuals. As the Finance Director General, I was responsible for ensuring that resources were used efficiently. The Policy Director Generals wanted to ensure their policies were implemented effectively. There was a strong mutual interest that the whole Department was viewed as effective and efficient. I was very happy to be described as the 'glue' that helped the team hold together and build something that was more than the sum of the parts.

When you have been able to contribute to the success of a team, every member of the team shares in the reflected glory. As you observe a good leader in action and share in team work that turns stretching initiatives into effective outcomes, you become more confident and assertive.

The more you see success as the success of the team rather than your contribution alone, the more you become aligned with other members of the team and willing to be generous in sharing resources, open to learning from your colleagues and able to rejoice in the shared endeavour that leads to good-quality outcomes.

Rashid put a lot of personal effort into a radical redesign of the training and development programmes for the global organisation. She enjoyed the people she was working with and wanted the team to gain full credit. She took pleasure in the way she had enabled some of the team to be more confident. She was pleased with her own contribution but did not want to shout about that. Focusing on the contribution of the team fitted well with her values.

Rashid was determined that the team received credit and that the credit was shared amongst all the team members. She was not seeking particular credit for her personal contribution. She talked openly in many different fora about the conclusions of the group, and became associated with the constructive outcomes of the whole team. Her performance assessment included positive words from the team leader of the project. Rashid got a lot of credit without seeking it for herself.

In practice

- Enjoy being part of a team and see team success as your personal success

- Observe how the success of the team rubs off on the reputation of individual members

- Build team success into your CV and your narrative about the contribution you bring

- Remember that pushing your own contribution too hard can undermine the success of the team

- Do not feel that you have to get credit for every contribution you make; your contribution will be observed in its entirety

69 ALLOW YOUR CONTRIBUTION TO EVOLVE OVER TIME

THE MOST EFFECTIVE CONTRIBUTION you can make to any team will evolve in the light of changing circumstances; do not allow your contribution to be frozen in time.

The idea

There is a risk in any team of sticking to a standard formula and not allowing the way the team works together to evolve. It is as if we are constrained to play a forehand shot when returning any tennis ball. Good tennis players are forever developing their repertoire so they can play the best shot in any situation.

In the early days of being a member of a committee, the most effective contribution might be a question or a short summary about progress so far. With greater experience, the authoritative team member is able to put forward a proposition which captures the essence of what needs to be done. Or the authoritative team member is bringing a perspective about potential outcomes and identifying a couple of key considerations which need to be resolved before effective progress can be made.

Your contribution to a team will also evolve in the light of the team's changing membership. As others join, you will want to give them space to develop their contribution and impact. You may want to stand back and let others move into other leadership roles. Your contribution might evolve from asking questions into putting forward propositions or into providing a wise sounding board about the likely reactions of different individuals and groups.

Rashid was delighted to have the opportunity to be part of an international group. Initially she was apprehensive and prepared in detail for every discussion. As time went on, she became more relaxed and more able to contribute on a wider range of issues.

Rashid developed an intuitive sense about what would work in the group and what would not, as well as a sensitivity about the likely reactions of people in different countries and in different sectors.

As Rashid became ever more relaxed with people who were older and more senior than her, she spoke with more humour. Her lightness of touch meant she became even more influential. In the early days, Rashid felt that she had to make her points strongly in order to be heard. As time went on, she recognised that a good contribution could be brief, catch people's imagination, be visual and give a flavour of what was possible.

In practice

- Never believe that you have reached perfection; continue to develop your approach

- Observe yourself to see how your impact and contribution changes over time within a team

- Allow yourself to keep widening your repertoire and try different approaches

- Allow your intuitive sense to inform the contributions you make

- Allow your contribution to become ever lighter in tone and be willing to touch on the humorous and tease your colleagues

- Keep seeking feedback from colleagues about whether your contributions are evolving in a helpful way

70 RECOGNISE WHEN IT IS TIME TO MOVE ON

WHEN EFFECTIVENESS DIMINISHES, the right thing may be to say, 'Thank you, I enjoyed that experience, and it is now time to move on and do something different'.

The idea

There is a life cycle for any committee and for your involvement in any team. The wise sportsperson knows when it is time to retire and let someone else move into the team. Most of us have observed people staying in a team for too long. Their effectiveness decreases and eventually they have to be 'invited' to leave.

When a term of office is for a defined number of years, leaving is not a problem, as it is an accepted part of the procedures. When a project team is set up for a particular purpose and is time-limited, there is less embarrassment about moving on from the project.

The best way of assessing the time to move on is a combination of listening to other people and to your own intuition. There may be occasions when others want you to move on prematurely because of the agenda they are taking forward. Sometimes it is diplomatic to leave to let the next generation take over; on other occasions, it is right to resist this suggestion as your continued presence brings a valued and important perspective that should not be lost.

When it is time to move on, it is important for your self-esteem that you are clear how you have contributed and what you have learnt from the experience. But as you end your engagement with one group or team, you will need to think about what is the next group or team you want to be part of. The sportsperson may move from playing to coaching. The nurse may move on from working with a group of nurses to being part of a team training new nurses. As we move on we take our experience and training with us, but the cycle begins again through the asking of questions and the finding of the best way of contributing to the effectiveness and impact of the next team you are part of.

Rashid was conscious that she had thoroughly enjoyed being part of the team looking at changes in training and development within the global organisation. Clear outcomes had been reached and were going to be implemented. There was going to be a Phase Two which she could have been part of but she thought the next phase needed different team members.

Rashid had learnt a lot through her participation in the team, developing much greater confidence in contributing at a corporate and international level. She wanted to bank that learning and explore how she could contribute as part of a different cross-cutting team. Next time round she wanted to be more confident and influential earlier. She had developed techniques that worked for her.

In practice

- See your participation in any team as having a beginning, a middle and an end

- Watch your emotions when your participation comes to an end; see it as a natural conclusion and not a painful transition

- Observe when your contributions are less needed or influential

- See the ending of participation in one team or committee as an opportunity to play a different part in another team

- Celebrate endings as much as beginnings

SECTION H
ENSURING EFFECTIVE TEAM DEVELOPMENT

71 HAVE A CLEAR PURPOSE AND BE REALISTIC ABOUT THE OUTCOMES OF TEAM EVENTS

TEAM EVENTS NEED A clear purpose combined with realism about outcomes if they are to be successful.

The idea

Team events have different purposes. If the objective is for team members to get to know each other better, the desired outcome might be the greater appreciation of each other's strengths, interests and experience, or an agreement to work in partnership on shared interests, or to draw on each other's strengths and experience more explicitly.

If the objective is to think through a strategic issue, the outcome might be agreement on three or four strands of work to be taken further forward by individuals or pairs.

If the objective is to look in some detail at a problem that is proving intractable, the outcome might be a series of actions with clarity about who is taking forward each action.

There is a risk of being either over-ambitious or too hesitant about outcomes. It may be much more important to reach a common mind about the direction of travel on some key areas of work, rather than using collective time to set out detailed actions. But if there are no outcomes, participants may feel the event has been of limited value.

The most effective team events often have just three or four key outcomes. The list is long enough to be worthwhile but short enough to be memorable. A long litany of actions that is unspecific about who takes responsibility is likely to be forgotten and ignored. If there is a list of actions, there needs to be clarity about who is accountable for taking forward each one.

Karen inherited a disparate team whose members were operating in silos. There was a sense of goodwill but not much mutual support. Karen's first step was to plan a half-day workshop with the team where they updated each other about what was happening in their areas and how they were seeking to develop their staff.

Karen's objective was limited to building mutual understanding and encouraging team members to adopt some good practices from other parts of the organisation. Each team member went away with more understanding of their colleagues' responsibilities and some ideas about using the talents of staff more fully.

In practice

- Be precise about the purpose of team events
- Think carefully about the outcomes you are seeking; make sure they are plausible, realistic and memorable
- See outcomes at different levels, including the emotional, rational and practical levels
- Seek to minimise any ambiguity about the reasons for an event, while letting an event flow with its own momentum
- Ensure the outcomes are clear, memorable, and recorded

72 USE EXTERNAL TEAM COACHING OR FACILITATION WISELY

GOOD-QUALITY EXTERNAL TEAM COACHING or facilitation can enable a team to reach a new level of awareness and focus, provided it does not detract from the accountability of individual team members.

The idea

Engaging an external coach or facilitator signals to the team that a team event is something different, i.e. it is not the usual weekly or monthly business meeting. Freed from chairing the event, the team leader can contribute as a member and offer more speculative ideas. A good team coach or facilitator will be observing the dynamics in the room and will be able to steer a conversation, or hold a mirror up to what is happening in the room.

A good external facilitator will ensure that every team member is able to contribute effectively and challenge them on the quality of their discussion and whether they are living the behaviours they aspire to.

By building a relationship of trust with each participant, the external coach will be able to draw them out in a way that ensures honest, open and effective dialogue, while staying mindful of where the team leader is coming from and checking with them about progress and next steps.

Karen invited an external coach to work with her team. The coach asked team members to talk about when the team had worked well and what had enabled that to happen. She then got the team to reflect on what had they learnt from what had gone less well. They talked about the type of team that they wanted to be in a few months' time and how they hoped members of the organisation would describe the team. Based on aspirational description the team reflected on the behaviours they would need to adopt so that people in the organisation would view them in the way they hoped.

In practice

- Be clear why you want to use an external team coach or facilitator and what contribution you want from such an individual

- Ensure clear contracting with the coach or facilitator

- Observe how the coach builds a relationship of trust with colleagues in the team, while keeping objectivity and distance

- Have an agreement about how you and the coach will communicate during an event so there can be flexibility in the way time is used

- Remember that you are in charge even though the coach or facilitator is managing the process

- Enable a relationship to be built between the team and the coach so that the team seek and respond to challenge from the coach

- Use an external coach or facilitator in order to differentiate an event from day-to-day business

73 CREATE REFLECTIVE SPACE

In a 24/7 world, it is all the more important to create space and time where team members can reflect and look at consequences and opportunities.

The idea

A team is judged by its outcomes. The focus is on productivity and performance. The drive for achievement can be relentless, with expectations becoming ever more demanding and short-term.

It is important to encourage individual team members, as well as the team as a whole, to take time to reflect. Some individuals reflect through creating space for conversation so that thoughts can be articulated and tested out. Others need quiet space in order to process their thinking. An effective team event will allow for a mix of approaches.

The confident team coach may encourage periods of silence when people note down their ideas or reactions. They may also encourage dialogue in pairs or threes. The encouragement to work through 'what if' scenarios can help a team see different possibilities and dangers ahead.

Creating reflective space might include suggesting a team meets in different locations, which might be as diverse as a monastery, an art gallery, or a private dining room. The chosen space might deliberately be free of tables, to encourage openness.

Karen decided that her team needed the stimulus of meeting in different contexts. They started one half-day by spending an hour looking at a David Hockney art exhibition. They then reflected on how the artist had drawn out moods through the use of colour and texture in different paintings. This led to a discussion about how they could draw out the themes and characteristics of the 'landscape' in which they were operating. The team had another half-day in a monastery and used that as a basis for thinking about building more simplicity and clarity into the work of their organisation, and how they might reduce some of the institutional clutter.

In practice

- Recognise how different people in your team best reflect

- Encourage reflection both individually and in the team as a whole

- Think through what type of reflection would be most helpful to the team and talk through with members of the team what they might experiment with

- Ensure that any external coach or facilitator builds reflection into the workshops or development days

- Experiment with using different locations to create different types of reflective space

- Encourage team members to be open about what type of reflective space brings out the best in them

74 MANAGE TIME AND ENERGY EFFECTIVELY

If TIME AND ENERGY are managed well, the commitment of team members will be enhanced and their resilience strengthened.

The idea

Time is finite, energy is variable. The days of expecting all team members to spend long hours at work for extended periods are gone, especially when both parents in a family are working. Energy levels can vary widely depending on how committed people are.

The best team events use time in a way that provides security about start and end points, while leaving flexibility about how time is used. They also recognise that energy levels vary and that energy can be lost quite quickly.

The person running a team event needs to be mindful of the time and periodically check with team members whether they are satisfied with the use of time. A good Chair uses breaks and encourages movement in the room in order to revive flagging energy levels.

Managing time well might mean deliberately taking some topics quickly, while allowing more reflection space for more strategic or complicated issues. The person chairing will have an eye to whose contributions can generate energy or sap energy in a room.

Karen was adept at introducing items at team meetings and events in such a way that people understood the nature of the discussion they were going to have. She set a tone and drew out expectations which steered participants in a way they recognised and responded to. She knew that she could use her tone of voice to uplift or quieten a conversation.

Karen deliberately used her subsequent interventions to influence the type of debate and the nature of the energy in the room. She was disciplined about building breaks into a meeting and encouraging people to sit in different places and speak in different sequences. She invited team members at the end of a meeting to comment on the extent to which they had used time effectively, and what had energised them or sapped their energy.

In practice

- See time as a precious commodity that is not to be wasted

- Ensure events start and end on time

- Deliberately vary the pacing of the way a team considers different issues, to provide variety and encourage different types of dialogue

- Observe energy levels and be mindful how they can be influenced by your tone of voice

- Encourage external feedback so that the team is aware of how its use of time and energy transmits to others

- Be mindful how a team can maintain energy over the longer term

75 ENCOURAGE PEOPLE TO THINK AND ACT OUT OF ROLE

IF TEAM MEMBERS are encouraged to think and act out of role, it can help build clarity about the perspectives of those they are working with, and lend a more purposeful edge to their approach.

The idea

A good organisation that wants to be responsive will encourage people to experience what it is like to be a customer or a client. The team member who has been a client will be much more sensitive to how the client is treated and what works best in terms of communication.

It helps a team member to be more effective if they can see issues from the perspective of other team members. If a new team member spends a day shadowing the finance lead, they are likely to develop a greater appreciation of funding and efficiency issues. If a team member within a Government organisation spends time in a school or hospital, they are much more likely to bring back to a team an appreciation of the impact that a team might have externally.

It will always be helpful for a team to think about what people's perceptions are of that team, and what evidence they would need to change that perspective.

Some teams have experimented with one team member describing in a wider meeting what another team member does. Other organisations have gone as far as enabling team members to swap roles for a couple of weeks so they have the accountabilities of another team member for a period.

Doing someone else's job within the team for a period creates greater awareness and can widen the repertoire of approaches a team member brings. When they sit in the job of someone they respect, some of the style and approach of the incumbent in the post will rub off on the person temporarily occupying the role. Someone who has admired a colleague's confidence is likely to embrace some of that confidence when occupying that person's role, even for a relatively short period.

Karen invited her team members to meet in pairs and talk in some depth about the joys and frustrations of the other person's role. Each team member also partnered with someone from another organisation to talk about what it was like in their respective roles. They then met as a group of four to talk about common themes and what they were learning from how each of them tackled similar dilemmas.

In practice

- Be willing to set an example by taking on different roles
- Be open to seeing issues from very different perspectives
- Encourage team members to see it as worthwhile to work-shadow people from different organisations
- Encourage people to articulate how an issue will be viewed by different groups of people
- Invite team members to work in pairs so they can speak on each other's behalf
- Encourage the setting up of informal learning sets with people in very different roles

76 USE FEEDBACK EXERCISES AND PSYCHOMETRIC ASSESSMENTS WITH CARE

THE RESULTS FROM feedback exercises and psychometrics can provide useful input but need to be considered as one input among many.

The idea

There is a risk that team events become data-free zones. There needs to be an awareness of how the team is perceived and an understanding about the preferences of individuals.

A valuable input to team events can be a summary of the perspectives of those who observe the team – clients, customers, sponsors, parallel organisations or staff. When people from these groups are asked for their opinions, what they say will reflect their own situation, hence there can be a colouring of their perspective. What is important is identifying a pattern within these views.

Collecting the perspectives of different players can be done by a trusted individual who is supporting the team or by an external analyst or coach. The basis for the collection of these perspectives needs to be set out clearly so that people understand whether it is the views of individuals or generic themes that are going to be fed back to the team.

Team members need some time to interpret the data that is presented to them so that they do not immediately go into defensive or aggressive modes. Psychometric data can provide a rich source of information to enable team members to understand each other better. As an example, MBTI can provide a useful matrix so people understand their differences and how they are likely to come over to their colleagues. As noted earlier, the more detailed MBTI Step II provides a particularly valuable disaggregation of the MBTI preference assessment.

Karen asked a coach who had been trained in MBTI Step II to lead a conversation with the team about their MBTI results. The discussion helped them understand who preferred to work through issues by talking about them, and who needed space and time to reflect. There were insights about the best frame of reference for some being to start with the big picture and then move to the details, whereas for others it was to start from the details and then move to the bigger picture. There were insights about the relative preferences of different individuals for forward planning and deciding in the moment.

In practice

- Be systematic in thinking through what external data about a team's impact will be useful

- Ensure the feedback is collected by someone who is trusted and objective

- Give space to enable people to reflect on feedback without having to rush to instant action

- Consider the use of psychometric assessments but don't expect them to give you all the answers

- See psychometric assessment results as one of a number of indicators and not as perfect evidence

77 RECOGNISE THE SIGNIFICANCE OF EMOTIONAL BONDS

EMOTIONAL BONDS BETWEEN members of a team give it strength and resilience but can potentially lead to a blindness to reality.

The idea

When there are shared objectives, a team can feel an emotional bond that leads to mutual support and encouragement. Success will create a sense of joy. If the team has taken action that was unsuccessful, there can be an emotional reaction of wanting to support each other or an emotional reaction of feeling let down by other team members.

The resilience of a team is rooted in mutual respect and an emotional bond between team members. When a team is working well together, the emotional bonds will enable a team to withstand shocks, handle disagreement and conflict, and come out of tough situations stronger.

If there is a breakdown of trust in a team and the emotional bonds are damaged, it can lead to an underlying unease and, potentially, resentment. If the emotional ties between members of a team are too strong, the team can risk losing objectivity, with people more concerned to defend each other rather than speaking truth about what is happening.

In a team event, it is worth observing the emotional inter-relationships between team members and noting whether they are beneficial or detrimental. After a successful event, reflect on the dynamics that were operating between team members and what they say about the relative quality of relationships.

If the team has not been successful, encourage a dispassionate conversation about the team members' emotional reactions and how best these can be used to good effect. Being honest about negative emotional reactions is never easy, but it makes a team more adaptable and effective going forward.

Karen decided towards the end of one team event to raise the issue of emotional links between team members. She invited members to talk about their emotions when they came to team meetings and how those emotions were affected by the attitude and contribution of others. She was open in her initial contribution about when she was encouraged or discouraged.

Karen talked about how her emotions were affected by the type of contribution and the tone of voice of other members. This led to a very candid conversation, with team members becoming more self-aware of the impact they had and how they might modify their approaches in order for the team to work more effectively.

In practice

- Be honest about your own emotional reactions at team meetings and in relation to the contributions of members

- Observe the emotional reactions of others both in team meetings and when they are interacting bilaterally

- Encourage team members to be honest about their emotional reactions and to share them

- Invite good-quality, reflective conversation after there has been disagreement so that people share their emotional reactions and how they have understood them and lived with them

78 EXPLORE SENSITIVE ISSUES

SENSITIVE ISSUES ARE OFTEN best explored when team members are in a more reflective mode and situation. But they still need careful preparation and handling.

The idea

There are some sensitive issues which it is right to 'park' and leave unspoken – relations may be too embryonic to risk progress by highlighting them. But the effectiveness of a team will be inherently limited if there are unspoken dimensions or undercurrents. The effective team leader will want to ensure that these issues do not fester.

If it is a politically sensitive issue, preparation in advance is important to ensure that there is no ambiguity about the facts, with all the key considerations being addressed in the preparation. A short note flagging up the issues rather than a long, detailed paper can be the best way of setting up a constructive conversation.

If the sensitive issue flows from very different personalities, the team leader may want to have bilaterals with the individuals first, or suggest that the individuals should meet in advance of a team discussion to see what progress they can make with each other.

An external team coach can play a key role in posing questions and then pressing for honest responses if people are reluctant to participate in addressing sensitive issues. A skilled team coach will know when to call 'time out' to enable people to reflect and decide whether to modify their stance.

If individuals are likely to be personally sensitive, it is important to set up a supportive context, which might mean a quiet environment or the expectation of a glass of wine at the end of the conversation.

Karen recognised there was a split in her team over a major priority. A lot of effort had been invested in a particular programme by some team members. Others were sceptical about its value. Previous discussions had been excessively polite or had been a bit cryptic, with strong views not spoken. Karen saw that there needed to be a frank discussion about this programme and whether it was worth continuing to invest funds in it. She talked to individual team members about the need for an open discussion.

Karen chose a venue outside the main office building. She set a tone of inviting people to reflect on the pros and cons. She started by asking a proponent and a critic of the programme to summarise where they thought the other person would be coming from. She steered an open conversation, pacing it quite slowly, and kept coming back to key points of evidence. Eventually there was agreement that the programme should continue but be focused on more limited outcomes.

In practice

- Be honest with yourself about what are the sensitive issues the team is finding it difficult to handle

- Ensure the best possible evidence is made available to inform you and colleagues about the sensitivities

- Be deliberate about the context and environment for the discussion of sensitive issues

- Prepare people carefully and chair the discussion thoughtfully, without having a predetermined view of the right outcome

79 MINIMISE DISTRACTIONS

THERE IS ALWAYS NOISE in people's minds and hearts. Seeking ways of 'parking' those distractions and minimising interference is part of effective planning for team events.

The idea

Distractions come in many different shapes and sizes. It can be movement outside the window, the rattle of coffee cups, the sound of voices, the vibration of the telephone, the rustling of papers or coughing and sneezing. There may be mental distractions caused by the memory of a difficult conversation, the telephone call that needs to be made, the e-mail that should have been written, the supper that needs to be bought, or the birthday card that should have been sent.

Good preparation for a team event includes thinking through what might be the distractions and how best they can be minimised. What are the ground rules about participation and the use of telephones? Can time slots for an event be clear so that there are gaps for any urgent clearances or brief calls?

It helps to ask participants to think what are the distractions that might affect them. Introduce a brief discussion about how best to ensure the team focuses on the agenda issue for the next hour; specify a length for the discussion, with a stock-take along the way.

Sometimes, if a conversation is getting bogged down, you might want to introduce a distraction deliberately in order to create a diversion or a lightness in the room. The distraction might be as simple as 'Let us break for coffee', or it might be to tell a story that is only partially relevant. The intent behind the distraction is to give people mental space to reflect and readjust their perspective.

Karen knew that important financial results were going to become available on the morning of the next team meeting. She was conscious that people's attention would be distracted by these figures. Her choice was either to ignore those figures, or to suggest that the team had a ten-minute reflection on those figures before moving into the intended agenda.

Karen thought it better to name the distraction and invite brief reflection with a commitment to a more substantive conversation the following week. In this way she enabled members of the team to feel that their initial concerns had been heard, and to have 'parked' this issue so it did not detract from the time that the team was spending together, and to then have space to reflect further.

In practice

- Recognise what is distracting you and be willing to name it to others

- Have an eye to what might be causes of distraction for others in the room

- Ensure that physical distractions are kept to a minimum, with clarity about the timings during the team event

- Be flexible enough to allow distractions to be named and discussed within a time-limited period

- Occasionally introduce a distraction as a deliberate ploy to give people time to think

- Recognise that unpredictable distractions happen and be willing to go with the flow before bringing a discussion back to its intended purpose

80 END ON A HIGH

IF A TEAM EVENT or meeting ends on a high, participants are much more likely to leave the room committed to take forward agreed steps with energy and persistence.

The idea

For some leaders, the team event is only worth the time commitment if the outcome is a set of detailed action points. For others, their apprehension about team events is that they will end up with a long set of actions. Any team event will have an outcome, but the outcomes might be more about personal engagement than specific action. If a team meeting sets off a particular train of thought then it is adding value.

You want participants to leave a team event in a positive frame of mind. They may be thoughtful and still working issues through. You want them to leave feeling purposeful and engaged in taking forward such issues.

It can help to imagine how participants will be describing a particular team event to a family member or friend after it has finished. What adjectives will they use to describe their feelings? It can sometimes be useful at the start of a meeting to ask people to reflect on how they want to leave the meeting, and then ask them at the end of the meeting whether the chosen phrase accurately describes how they are leaving a meeting.

Leaving on a high is not about excessive jollity; it is about the discussion having been worthwhile, leading to a greater sense of working together, with clarity about next steps. A thank you from the Chair can lead to a smile and increase the prospect of team members wanting to be back in each other's company again.

Karen was conscious that the team had worked hard to think through relative priorities. Team members had recognised the concerns of other members of the team and had been willing to compromise.

Karen decided to be explicit in her concluding comments in thanking team members for the way they had entered the conversation. She referred to the values that team members had demonstrated. She recognised that some members of staff in wider teams might feel unhappy about the outcome and acknowledged that team members were going to need to give consistent and potentially unwelcome messages.

Karen deliberately closed the meeting by referring to a couple of examples where earlier decisions taken by the team had proved to be right and had led to public acknowledgement for the work of the team. Karen wanted the team members to leave what had been a demanding conversation feeling that there was a consistent track record of good decisions with good outcomes.

In practice

- Think ahead about how you want a meeting to end
- Anticipate how people are likely to leave the room and recognise the scope you have to influence that mood
- Ensure that the conclusions of a discussion are clear so that people leave the event feeling there has been progress
- Express thanks to key people so the meeting ends with a tone of appreciation
- End on an informal note, with a smile

SECTION I
ENSURING TEAMS KEEP LEARNING

81 ENCOURAGE BRIEF STOCK-TAKES AT THE END OF MEETINGS

IT IS ALWAYS WORTH spending a few minutes at the end of a meeting doing a stock-take about the conclusions, alongside reflecting on what worked well and what worked less well.

The idea

At the end of a meeting, there is a risk that the Chair assumes that his or her understanding of the conclusions is identical to that of the other participants. Even if the Chair tries to summarise the conclusions and actions required, it may be done in a rushed way with limited clarity. The ideal is that, say, five minutes before a meeting ends, the Chair makes clear the conclusions and who is doing what as next steps.

Equally useful at the end of a meeting is a brief review of what went well or less well. This rarely gets 'above the line', but if the approach and behaviour in one meeting is going to inform what happens in the next meeting, some reflective moments at the end of meetings is desirable.

Reviewing what went well reinforces good practice. Asking what went less well is a more demanding question – one that can create a wall of silence. It can be helpful to focus the question through asking, 'What one thing might we do differently next time?' Participants are usually more willing to answer a specific question than to give an overview. This approach creates a more engaged discussion.

A variation is to invite one member prior to a meeting to reflect at the end on how the meeting went. If this role moves around members of the team, a pattern can be reinforced about giving brief but thoughtful feedback.

Helen had originally taken over leading the leadership team in a Government office. She had been welcomed by members of the team but felt their approach was a bit predictable and staid. The team meetings covered the ground efficiently but were neither challenging nor innovative.

Her first step was to invite members of the team at the end of her second team meeting to discuss what went well and less well in their meeting. She wondered if they would be complacent. Although there was quite a lot of self-congratulation, there was an acknowledgment in their comments that they did not make the best use of their time. They suggested there was scope for a greater degree of questioning about the way things had always been done. Helen felt she had begun to open up the possibility of greater self-awareness and learning going forward.

In practice

- Ensure that the conclusions of a meeting are always clear and understood

- Be explicit about the need for some defined, if brief, time to agree conclusions and action points

- Signal the value of periodic reviews at the end of team meetings about what has gone well or less well

- Be frank in sharing your own views; warn people in advance that this is what you are going to do and do not spring it on them

82 ENCOURAGE THE ARTICULATION OF OBSERVATION AND FEEDBACK

EXTERNAL OBSERVATION AND FEEDBACK can be very insightful – what is good or less good may not be apparent to all members.

The idea

When you are at home in a team, you do not always observe critically what is going on. You have got used to the foibles of individuals and to the way conversations unfold. You have developed an acceptance of the limitations in the way options are considered.

Inviting someone to observe a team and provide feedback can be a powerful intervention. The observer who has not been part of this team meeting before will come with fresh eyes, be able to pick out strengths that team members have taken for granted, and identify emotions that team members have become immune to.

External observers will see the interactions between people and recognise what type of interventions would be influential. They will observe when energy levels go up or down. They may be able to pinpoint moments when there is a change of direction, and when there is acceptance about a course of action, or a growing resistance to a previously assumed way forward.

The observer's views have to be treated with caution, as the individual may know little about the context or the interpersonal dynamics. Not all their comments will be right, but the neutral observer will inevitably say some truths that need to be said and provide pointers for future action.

Feedback needs to be received courteously and seriously, and then reviewed carefully before action is taken. If team members look defensive when feedback is given, this reaction will be a source of gossip around the organisation. The signalling of an openness to feedback and a willingness to act in response to it will cascade constructively through an organisation if a team treats feedback with the interest and respect it deserves.

Helen decided to invite a bright junior member of staff from her office and a middle manager from an adjacent office to attend a team meeting. Their brief was to observe and not speak during the meeting. At the end, they were invited to express their comments on strengths and development areas. The comments were respectful and questioning.

There were observations about the extent to which people listened in an engaged way to their colleagues. There were questions about how members might have moved the discussion on constructively and identified points of agreement earlier. What was powerful from these observations was the combination of a junior member of staff who had had no experience of such teams and a middle manager who had worked in similar teams in other localities. The fact that many of their comments overlapped meant that the team took their observations seriously.

The team leader was careful to agree with the team members which three points were the ones they wanted to take forward in the way they worked together. Helen was conscious that if there were too many action points none would get done.

In practice

- Prepare team members for external observation and feedback; do not spring it on them

- Start off by choosing an observer that the team already knows and trusts

- Experiment with inviting different types of people from inside and outside the organisation to observe and give feedback

- Remember that the views of junior staff and younger people can often be very valuable as they may spot obvious points that others have become immune to

- Ensure that action following feedback is focused and limited to a manageable number of points

- Always remember that any observer's feedback says as much about the individual as the content of the feedback

83 ENCOURAGE MEETINGS TO TAKE PLACE IN DIFFERENT CONTEXTS AND DIFFERENT FORMULATIONS

IF MEETINGS ARE HELD IN different places and in different combinations of participants, they can generate freshness, liveliness and creativity.

The idea

Some organisations have adopted the practice of holding brief meetings standing up. A space may be set aside for such meetings that includes high pedestal tables. Stand-up meetings generate an expectation that they will not be long. Participants will, after a while, not be enjoying standing up and will be more willing to agree action going forward in order to bring the meeting to an end.

Sometimes the opposite type of stimulus is needed. Relaxing in an armchair provides reflective space, allowing team members to open up about their uncertainties or vulnerabilities.

A team leader may well be making a conscious decision when someone enters their space about whether they talk around a table, or standing up, or seated in informal chairs. There is no right or wrong answer; it all depends what type of discussion the team leader is seeking to promote, what conclusions they want to work towards and for how long they want the discussion to last.

The normal assumption is that team meetings are always in plenary, but it can be valuable to split up a discussion so some of it is in pairs, or threes, or in two groups. Using different formulations encourages the quieter members to speak. It enables them to articulate their perspectives, which can then be crystallised and fed back into the wider consideration.

If a team meets near the place or the people they are seeking to influence, they are much more likely to build an understanding of what it feels like to be the recipient or customer. A team from a national headquarters that meets at the site of a subsidiary will learn far more about that subsidiary in its locality than they would by meeting a couple of representatives in the headquarters office.

Helen observed that members of her team always sat in the same places around the table, which reinforced the predictability of what they did and said. Helen varied the place where she sat. When they were planning to have a meeting about longer-term issues, Helen suggested they meet in a different building. She requested that chairs be laid out in a circle with no central table, creating a very different atmosphere from being seated around a rectangular table. She ensured that for some of the topics they split into smaller groups, with a limited time for headline themes to be fed back to the full team.

Helen arranged for one of the meetings to be in a community centre located well away from their clinical offices. On another occasion, the team met in a private room of a hotel. Helen was deliberately bringing in changes to stimulate freshness of conversation and thought.

In practice

- Observe what is predictable in the way meetings happen
- Encourage some stand-up conversations and short meetings, being mindful of any health and well-being issues

- Choose different locations for some of the meetings and observe the relationship between the location and the emotions in the room

- Deliberately vary the layout of a room; remove tables wherever possible so they are not a barrier to quality interaction

- Encourage conversation about the relationship between the productivity of a team and the different contexts they are in

- Remember to vary the formulations and use dialogue in pairs or threes as well as plenary

84 ENCOURAGE INPUT FROM A RANGE OF SPECIALISTS

Using an 'expert witness' approach can provide new insights and help ground a team's consideration of complex issues so the next actions are realistic and bold.

The idea

In any area of activity, there will be specialists who have knowledge and experience that it is right to draw on. It is important, however, to define the scope of that input so it does not become overwhelming.

Views about legal constraints provide a valuable framework. But legal precedent is not always the end of the story. Sometimes the views of specialists have to be recognised as coming from a blinkered perspective. For example, a cautious accountant will tell you about all the pitfalls. What is needed is the expertise of an accountant to both forewarn you of risks and help provide solutions about a productive way forward.

The IT specialist will be passionate in their advocacy. You have to draw on their expertise in order to keep your organisation and team up to date, but their expectations about the timetable for transformation may need to be treated with considerable caution.

What matters is building trust in those whom you bring in so that they fully recognise that they will only be taken seriously if their evidence is grounded and substantiated. Never be afraid of specialists; always be willing to ask them obvious questions. When they begin to use unfamiliar language, stop them and ask them to keep things clear and simple.

Helen asked a specialist in operational management to talk to a team about changes they had developed in a similar type of organisation in a different sector. Helen's steer to the specialist was to share two or three clear examples and to ensure that she caught the imagination of the team members. One stipulation was no jargon or management speak. As soon as the specialist began to talk in technical language, Helen brought the conversation back to a more practical level. She ensured that every team member was involved in the discussion and that agreement at the end was limited to a small number of deliverable changes.

On another occasion, Helen brought in a trainer who was a specialist in developing coaching skills in managers. The trainer encouraged the team members to believe that they used coaching approaches in their day-to-day lives and drew out the questioning skills they already applied. The trainer helped them recognise that they used coaching skills with their children which were equally applicable in the work situation.

In practice

- Experiment using an 'expert witness' approach so people share experience and expertise

- Be open to a range of different specialists from different backgrounds being expert witnesses

- Invite different types of specialists, with the understanding that their views are not automatically accepted but intelligently questioned and reflected upon

- Seek solutions which are informed – but not inhibited – by specialists

- Let the specialists go away feeling they have been taken seriously and are themselves better informed by the dialogue

85 ENSURE THE VOICE OF THE CUSTOMER IS NEVER FAR AWAY

THE TEAM THAT OPERATES in a vacuum with no regard for the customer is going to be short-lived, hence the importance of taking the views of the customer seriously.

The idea

A team must be clear who their customer is. Who is the paying client? Whose views will raise or tarnish the reputation of the team? Who is judging what success is and what that looks like? The 'customer is king', whether we like it or not.

Engaging the customer at the heart of the enterprise limits the risk of irrelevance and unwanted outcomes. A good team will invite the customer into the team, either to be part of it or to represent the customer's views directly. The good team will want evidence of the views and decisions of customers on a regular basis.

Customers who feel ignored will take their buying power and interest elsewhere. Customers who are not taken seriously will complain and rapidly damage the reputation of a team or organisation. The perception of your success is based on your last victory, hence the importance of continually investing in knowing what the customer wants and adjusting what the team does as a consequence.

The customer may not be right. Your customer might be the Marketing Director, but what actually matters are the decisions of purchasers rather than the views of the Marketing Director. When someone is in an intermediary role representing customers, it is important to have evidence that their views are representative and up-to-date.

The forward-looking team leader will have in their mind a range of different customers and be willing to seek the perspectives of different types of customers. They will always treat intermediary customers with caution while recognising the power that they often hold.

It can help to have team members talking on a regular basis to different customers, and then sharing their learning with colleagues. A central person can then identify trends from these conversations and ensure that the team has the evidence on which they can consider whether they need to change course.

Helen was concerned that some of her team members were not encouraging fresh thinking enough in their parts of the organisation. She promoted conversation about how the views of customers might best be understood. This involved talking to members of the public in a more open and less transactional way. For some members of the organisation, this was a big shift.

Helen decided to spend two half-days sitting with customers seeking their views. She was particularly impressed with three of the customers and invited them to join a meeting of the team and share their perspectives. These three individuals were not particularly articulate, but they were passionate about what worked and did not work for them. It was the persuasiveness in their tone and the colour of their language that convinced members of the team that they needed to find better ways of understanding where such customers were coming from.

In practice

- Encourage discussion about who is the customer and how their views are understood

- Recognise that some customers are only proxies for others

- Be willing to use innovative ways of sitting with customers and understanding what their needs and preferences are

- Invite customers into team meetings even though they may well not understand the norms and expectations of the way the team interacts internally

- Recognise that the customer is often right, even though they are not following your preferences

- Think through when a customer preference might be a passing fad rather than a long-term trend

86 ENCOURAGE INTERCHANGEABILITY OF ROLES WHERE POSSIBLE

ONCE PEOPLE HAVE TAKEN ON different roles in a team, they are much more likely to be willing to act corporately on behalf of the team and more likely to understand others' perspectives.

The idea

Team members who have held responsibilities in policy, finance, HR and operations will bring a breadth of experience and understanding that is far greater than if they had held only one role. A growing focus on individuals bringing specialist skills has tended to limit the opportunities for individuals to be in a range of different roles. But the more team members can appreciate what it is like to do the job of other people in the team, the more likely they are to think forward with a perspective from the whole team rather than just bringing a single perspective.

The good team leader will encourage members to develop their experience and qualifications so they can take on a wider range of responsibilities. The good team leader will ask individuals to take on different roles and projects, and potentially swap responsibilities.

When one team member is away for an extended period oversight of their responsibilities can be given to another team member. This can help build interchangeability and a greater awareness of the dynamics in different parts of the team's overall work.

Confident team leaders may ask other members of the team to do their job or part of their job when they are away. Creating a situation where team members feel they can do the team leader's job creates a confidence that they are not completely dependent on the team leader being present.

Helen wanted to break down the silo thinking that happened too often in the team. She sounded out two team members about doing a job swap for a couple of months so they understood each other's area better. They were initially hesitant, but with some reluctance agreed to swap for a month. They both felt unsettled for the first week but gradually appreciated the opportunity to understand more about the wider organisation and to develop their leadership approach in areas where they had little prior knowledge.

This experience helped both team members appreciate that their skills were more transferable than they realised and that they could pick up key issues reasonably quickly. They now understood the operational issues that both teams faced. After the swap period, the team members would talk more often about current issues and use each other as sounding boards. The swap, painful at the time, had long-term benefits.

In practice

- Draw on examples of people benefiting from switching roles
- Encourage professional development that enables people to become more adaptable and better equipped to take on different roles
- Encourage short-term swaps and rotation of responsibilities
- Create an expectation that responsibilities will move around so that team members take the initiative in suggesting possible switches

87   SEE CHANGING MEMBERSHIP AS AN OPPORTUNITY RATHER THAN A PROBLEM

A CHANGE IN MEMBERSHIP allows the team to be refreshed through new approaches and ideas. It prompts others in the team to think through the contribution they are making.

The idea

The initial reaction when an experienced person announces that he or she is moving on from your team can be one of gloom. You have grown dependent upon that individual's contribution and influence. But changing membership is inevitable. People need to move on and use their knowledge elsewhere. Others need to get the benefit of their expertise and insights.

You may feel that the hole left by that person is massive and difficult to fill. But there is an opportunity to bring in a new person with a different perspective and experience. You will be the one making the appointment, so the new person will want to do the best for you and you will be committed to their success.

As you look for a new team member, you are seeking someone who brings the right level of experience, expertise and attitude. You want somebody who can blend well with other members of the team and provide a contribution that stimulates the whole team to do well. This might be an opportunity to bring into the team a younger and less experienced person with a perspective from a different generation. Alternatively, you may be looking for someone who is older to help ground a team of younger people.

It is helpful to see the arrival of a new team member as an opportunity to put time and effort into developing the team as a whole. Existing team members may be more self-conscious about the way they work with a new team member and may, therefore, be more willing to try new ways of working and more willing to seek to develop the effectiveness of the whole team with new intent.

Helen's most experienced team leader was going to be retiring in three months. She wanted to ensure that the new recruit was appointed early enough for there to be some handover with the existing leader. She also wanted to appoint someone who was much more attuned to using modern technology effectively.

Helen wanted to use the new appointment as a means of getting the team to think in a new way about the future. At the same time, she wanted the person who was retiring to pass on his insights to the new appointee and do some mentoring of other team members before departing. She ensured a warm send-off for the retiring team member and put in the diary a half-day workshop for the new team three weeks after the new team member took up his post. The intent was to take stock of progress made and to review how they were going to bring out the best in each other as a team going forward.

In practice

- Accept that a continuous turnover of people in a team is more likely to be a benefit than a disadvantage

- Invest time in recruiting for both expertise and attitude

- Use the arrival of a new member to get the whole team to think about how it is going to work together going forward

- Be open-minded about the type of person and contribution you would want to see in a new team member

88 LEVERAGE THE BENEFITS OF WORKING VIRTUALLY

WORKING VIRTUALLY has huge benefits for the effective use of time and other resources, but there can be an inhibition about moving purposefully in this direction.

The idea

There is often the mindset that teams only work effectively if they are all in a room together. Some governance arrangements prohibit people participating in committees at a distance.

To global organisations, such inhibitions seem bizarre. Many organisations have become entirely attuned to using virtual communication adeptly. Once individuals get used to telephone meetings, video conferencing or Skype meetings, these platforms work almost as effectively as do face-to-face meetings.

The handling of virtual meetings needs particular care as the Chair cannot always see participants' facial expressions or experience their body language in the same way as in a face-to-face conversation. Checking in with people about how they are feeling about a subject and being clear about the conclusions become all the more important in virtual meetings.

Different team members will be more or less comfortable with virtual team working. An openness needs to be cultivated so people are able to talk about what is working or not working for them and able to experiment in different ways. There need to be thoughtful conversations about the balance of face-to-face and virtual meetings and what subjects are discussed where.

The more virtual the interaction, the more important it is to have face-to-face conversations that cover longer-term strategic issues and provide an opportunity for team members to talk openly about what is working for them or not working in their interchanges. It can be helpful to ask people to share their experiences of how they pick up signals from others when they are not in the same room and how best to encourage an open development of ideas in virtual meetings.

Two of Helen's team wanted to work at home one day a week. Helen saw advantage in the team leaders having more undisturbed space to work through complicated issues. She was also conscious that other members of the team might feel that the two team members working at home were 'getting an easy life'.

Helen wanted to establish that when people were working at home they were working and available, hence she deliberately organised some team conversations when these colleagues were working at home. Initially there was some unease about conducting a telephone meeting but gradually people got used to this type of exchange. There was an acceptance that participants were often more efficient in their use of words in telephone meetings, so that meetings were shorter and decisions taken faster.

In practice

- Talk with people who operate virtual teams to gain from their experience

- Be open to trying different approaches and observe what works well or less well

- Encourage people to learn from the experience of others and to share their frustrations about operating virtually

- Maintain a balance between virtual and face-to-face exchanges

89 | PARTNER TEAMS IN OTHER ORGANISATIONS

PARTNERING A TEAM in another organisation can provide valuable insights about team dynamics and effectiveness.

The idea

Sometimes it is operationally imperative to build a strong partnership with teams in other organisations. The finance team in a Government department needs to build a strong relationship with the relevant sponsor team in the Treasury or Finance Department. The sponsorship team in a national charity needs to have a good partnership with the leadership team in a region. The need for good-quality interaction between such teams is obvious but can be difficult if there are different priorities or long-standing frustrations.

To work well together, teams need to build transparent working arrangements that allow issues to be surfaced and resolved. Where there is an undercurrent of mistrust or scepticism, good-quality partnerships will be much more difficult to establish.

A key question is, 'What teams should we partner where there is an operational benefit in doing so?' A second question might be, 'Which teams can we partner where building up a mutual understanding will help both teams be more effective?' This might mean partnering a team doing a parallel job in the same organisation, or it might mean partnering a team in a different type of organisation with whom there are various parallels.

There are always insights that can be drawn from how a very different group of people approaches a similar set of issues. As a result of sharing stories, there are always going to be some ideas that can be transferred across. But the main benefits might flow purely from the conversation, as team members articulate what they do and why they do it.

Helen had built up links with a commercial organisation in the same town which had regular contact with customers. She recognised there were common themes in the work of the two teams about ensuring good-quality customer service. She agreed with her opposite number in this commercial team that there would be potential benefit in sharing experiences.

Members of both teams were initially sceptical. The first step was to visit each other's venues to understand the work that was done and the pressures that people were under. When the two teams met, some members gave presentations about issues they had faced and opportunities they had taken forward. Some of the considerations were different, including the financial drivers, but overall there were more similarities than differences. They shared examples of keeping up the motivation of staff through difficult times and of handling blips in the performance of individuals. There was good mutual learning about handling both changes and people.

In practice

- Look for teams in organisations where there is an operational need to build good-quality understanding and links

- Look for teams in organisations where there might be some parallels where there can be mutual learning

- Legitimise time being spent on building relationships with other teams

- Recognise that learning may be more about attitudes and approaches than detailed, specific measures

90 MERGE TEAMS TO GALVANISE PROGRESS

TEAMS CAN BECOME COMPLACENT. Merging teams keeps people alert, ready to learn from each other, and bolder going forward.

The idea

When I was a member of a national board that merged with another board, we had an imperative to be clear what the new organisation was responsible for and what its priorities were going to be. The merging of the two teams created focus and energy. Some of the existing roles would not exist after the initial weeks, but there was a shared purpose to get the new organisation established. Progress was galvanised even though there was going to be personal pain.

Sometimes a team might become predictable and stale over time. A sense of adventure has been lost or its area of responsibility has shrunk. Merging two teams forces the team leader to be clear on the direction and requires all the team members to think through and articulate what their contribution is going to be. Clear expectations can be put on a merged team to ensure they make the best of each other's talents and are clear on the values that are going to operate within the team.

Merging is not done for the sake of throwing up the pieces to see where they land; it is about recognising that disturbance is likely to lead to innovation and creativity if reasons are set out clearly and there is opportunity to talk through reactions and opportunities. When teams have been merged, reviewing progress after a while can help participants recognise the benefits and value of the new platform that has been created.

Helen inherited two teams doing similar tasks covering different geographical areas. Both teams were jolly and a bit cosy. The team members knew each other well and were a touch complacent. Helen decided that merging the two teams would mean they had to sharpen their way of thinking and be more open to listening and learning.

The sceptics talked about the inefficiency of a larger team and the difficulty of reaching conclusions in this size of group. Helen listened but persevered with her intent. She recognised the pros and cons of different sizes of teams. She was deliberately creating change in order to get people to think more carefully about what they were doing and why they were doing it. Helen thought it highly likely that some new ideas would come out of this process and that there would be a renewed freshness in the team discussions. Helen recognised that some people would find this transition more difficult than others, but she was prepared to pay the price.

In practice

- When a team has had the same functions and membership for a number of years, be mindful how effective and innovative it is

- Never assume a team structure is permanent

- Be clear of the potential merits of merging teams – they might be more about galvanising energy than creating a new perfect structure

- Encourage participants to see the merging of teams as a development opportunity for themselves

ENSURING CONTINUOUS LEARNING ABOUT LEADING TEAMS WELL

91 BELIEVE IN YOUR PROGRESS SO FAR

WHEN YOU BELIEVE IN the progress you have made, you are much more likely to move confidently and with ease into leading a team going forward.

The idea

As you walk up a steep hill, it can feel like hard work. When you stop, turn around and see the distance you have travelled and the height you have reached, there can be a quiet sense of satisfaction. Your resolve is renewed to walk further up the hill. It does not help to look back too frequently though. The risk then is that you will not feel you are making any progress.

As a team leader, it is not indulgent to review the team's progress. Progress may be measured by the outcomes delivered, or by the level of engagement within a team. Note down the outcomes a team has delivered and the progress it has made in the way it works together. It reminds the team that its progress has been the result of hard work and constructive thought. Allowing ourselves the time to be pleased about the progress made helps cement the belief that progress has been worthwhile and well earned.

Mike was the Head Teacher of a large secondary school. The team he inherited was dysfunctional; the first couple of years were hard work. Following some new appointments and his working closely with all the team members, it was now much more effective.

There was still a long way to go but Mike recognised that he was now a lot better at deciding when to draw in his team and when to act alone; when to give direct messages to his senior staff and when to stand back. The senior staff team meetings were more creative and dynamic, with constructive outcomes. Mike took a quiet satisfaction in observing the team engaging much better than the team he had inherited two years ago.

In practice

- Take time to note down the progress your team has made

- Reflect on how the way you lead the team has evolved

- Assess the extent to which you vary and pace your contributions more effectively than you did a year earlier

- Believe in your own progress, while recognising the support you have received from others

92 RECOGNISE THE ANXIETIES YOU CAN LEAVE BEHIND

ANXIETIES GET IN THE WAY of our continuous development. When we recognise them and seek to minimise them, there can be a liberation enabling good progress.

The idea

Our anxieties might have been good for us, helping us get to where we are. A fear of failure might have given us the drive and determination to work harder at building a team. Concern about our reputation might have meant that we worked hard to build alliances and partnerships with others. Doubts about our own ability might have meant seeking advice from trusted others and carefully weighing up different possibilities before making a decision.

A certain degree of anxiety keeps us alert to possibilities, mindful of risks and sensitive to the energy and motivational levels of those around us. But a preoccupation with our anxieties saps our energies and holds us back from levels of attainment and impact that we would otherwise have reached.

Anxieties need to be named, understood and boxed. We can thank our anxieties to the extent that they have helped us reach where we currently stand. Some anxieties will always be with us, but the more we can limit their effect and leave them behind the better.

The antidote for the fear of failure is recalling the progress made. The treatment for the fear of being found out is a track record of success. The corrective to being captured by nervous tension might be to pace your contribution in a more measured and deliberate way.

Mike was conscious that in the early hours of the morning he could be anxious about decisions he needed to make. He would play out, at great length, different ways of handling a conversation. He had made many difficult decisions, but when he was tired any decision could begin to feel disproportionately huge.

Mike recalled decisions he had made that eventually worked out for the best, even though the affected individuals were very critical at the time. He was conscientious in weighing up the evidence before making a difficult decision. He applied his values consistently and recognised that it was part of his job to make choices.

Over time, Mike limited the corrosive effect of his anxieties and managed to leave them behind on most occasions. When they reappeared, he reminded himself that a touch of anxiety kept him on his toes.

In practice

- Name the anxieties that cause you most concern
- Accept that these anxieties have sometimes helped you focus the use of your time and energy
- Be willing to talk through your anxieties and their effect on you
- Observe how others have handled similar anxieties effectively
- Recall evidence from previous occasions when anxiety was ill-founded
- Say 'Thank you for your insight' to your anxiety and move on

93 ACCEPT THAT YOU SHOULD NOT BE TRYING TOO HARD

WHEN WE TRY TOO HARD, we exhaust both ourselves and those around us.

The idea

We want to excel at being a team leader. We are willing to put in a lot of preparation, and having thought through all the next steps, we are ready to lead a team. However, when team members see us trying very hard to foresee any eventuality, they may conclude that they do not need to be particularly committed to the team. If your focus veers into doing the work of the whole team, their level of commitment may become low or dormant. When you try too hard, there is no room for the contribution of others.

Your intensity can also have the effect of pushing people away. They may be reluctant to enter your space. Instead, you want to draw team members into your thinking rather than force your thinking down their throats. You need to bring a lightness and a quality of engagement into your leadership of the team so they are attracted to you and want to support you and help deliver what is important to you.

Good team leaders are not trying too hard to deliver as individuals. They focus on steering the team and enabling members to grow in confidence and effectiveness. They are not spending too much time setting prescriptive boundaries. They foster an atmosphere of encouragement, which leads to a natural desire to go to the next level in contributing effectively to the team.

Throughout his career Mike had been pushing boundaries. He

brought a determination to his leadership. He always spoke very positively and persuasively about what was possible. There was an intensity in him that attracted some and repelled others.

Mike was conscious that he needed to moderate his intensity with some of his senior staff. He wanted to encourage some of his younger leaders to be curious about what might be possible and to draw on best practice from other schools. Mike accepted, intellectually, that he must not try too hard to provide the 'right' solution. He needed to encourage these younger leaders to develop curriculum approaches and ways of working that would stimulate staff and students. Mike stood back from his desire for perfection in order to legitimise innovation.

In practice

- Accept that trying hard is a strength you bring that has led to successful outcomes

- Be mindful that trying too hard can sap your energy and creativity

- Deliberately reduce the emphasis on trying very hard yourself and assess what other approaches, involving working through others, might be effective for you

- Consider the positive consequences of reducing the intensity of your contribution by, say, 50%

- Regard enabling others as a more important measure of success than delivering outcomes yourself

94 RECOGNISE WHAT IS THE STRETCH FOR YOU

I T I S W O R T H R E A S S E S S I N G, on a periodic basis, what is the development that you need to do next and what is the stretch that is going to be most demanding on you.

The idea

Our attitude to our own development as a team leader might get stuck in time. We may keep saying to ourselves that what I need to do better is strategic thinking, or making speeches, or chairing meetings. When we have logged the progress we have made, we need to re-evaluate, realistically, what is the next phase of required development. Once we have become better at speaking in front of a group of 50 people, we need to recognise our progress with this capability and consider what should be the focus of the next phase of development.

You might be about to enter a difficult period of negotiation, hence the importance of being realistic about the demands this will put on you, and then being practical about how best to develop your confidence and competence in handling demanding negotiations well.

Mike recognised that the stretch for him was revitalising and reorganising the design and technology area. The department had excelled ten years earlier but was now staid and unimaginative. There had been little movement in the staff and many seemed set in their ways. The department's past reputation had enabled it to attract good students, but their progress had only been moderate in recent years.

Mike knew that he had to face up to the senior staff of the department the reality that they were bordering on becoming a failing department. He needed to create the conditions whereby a couple of staff would be willing to retire, with the department bringing a much more dynamic approach to curriculum development and teaching approaches. He prepared himself for difficult conversations and knew it would take time to ensure willing progress.

Part of Mike's preparation was to recognise the progress he had made in other areas and to withdraw deliberately from some activities where the momentum was now self-generating. Mike talked through his next steps with two key members of his wider leadership team and ensured he had their support.

In practice

- Be as clear as you can in defining where you need to put your time and energy

- Recognise which of these activities will give you energy and which will sap your energy

- Acknowledge that in some areas you can lead your team without expending too much energy, while in other areas you will be stretched

- Be clear what are the hard issues you need to grasp and be willing to 'steel yourself' to do so

- Be realistic about how many stretching issues you can take on at any one time

- Ensure you have the support of key team members when you have to focus on difficult issues

95 ACCEPT THAT THERE WILL BE FALLOW PERIODS

THERE WILL BE TIMES when you make good progress and times when you and the team seem becalmed or static. Often these periods have to be lived through and accepted, until they come to a natural end.

The idea

If life moved continually forward at high speed, you and your team would be exhausted. If the team is involved in frenetic activity with no time to reflect, it is likely to become drained, bored and unimaginative.

Teams need fallow periods to draw breath and be able to survive over the longer term. Fallow periods are not wasted. Team members will still be processing their experience subconsciously. Their relationships with each other will continue to be evolving even when the intensity of activity is reduced.

During these periods, the team can be developing ways of working and levels of mutual understanding that become embedded and generate a conditioned way of working, ready for when it is called upon to move into a higher level of activity.

Fallow periods are good provided they do not go on for too long, and provided there continue to be an alertness to the changing environment and a desire to keep learning.

As a team leader, fallow periods can be a time of strengthening your understanding with different team members through a growing sensitivity towards each other's preferences. You become better equipped to work well with them when activity picks up again.

Mike could see that the forthcoming school year could appear like a fallow year. His leadership team was established. Priorities for the next couple of years were set. There was a good demand for places at the school, so the finances would be reasonably predictable. There were no immediate crises on the horizon.

Mike's reaction was to recognise that a fallow year would allow him and his senior team to build a deeper mutual understanding about the issues the school would need to address over the next three or four years because of demographic and economic changes. A fallow year would also mean that he could spend more time mentoring his senior staff, enabling them to consolidate their learning and think about the next steps in their careers.

In practice

- Recognise the value of fallow periods for both you and your team

- See the opportunities in fallow periods to take stock of learning and plan for the future

- Do not complain to yourself about fallow periods; recognise that levels of activity vary and can be unpredictable

- Allow yourself to enjoy a period where there are neither crises nor huge opportunities

- Recognise that fallow periods come to an end and be ready for the surprises or opportunities that ensue

96 RECOGNISE WHAT YOU CAN ACHIEVE WHEN YOU ARE AT YOUR BEST

RECOGNISING WHAT YOU CAN ACHIEVE when you are at your best provides a standard to aim for that will keep you motivated in tough periods.

The idea

A worthwhile question to ask team members about your contribution as leader is, 'When I am at my best, what am I doing?' Such an open-ended question invites your colleagues to say what they observe in the way you lead a team. Their comments are likely to be both about the content of what you say and the demeanour with which you lead. What people say they notice gives you valuable clues about the ways in which you impact most effectively on others.

When I was in my early 30s and leading a large division for the first time, my boss described the way I led my leadership team as purposeful, using their talents to best effect. This comment enabled me to understand more about what I was doing when I was at my best. That affirmation assisted me in building my own confidence and my belief that we, as a team, could lead and implement major reform in the financing of education.

Asking yourself the question, 'If I am at my best in leading this team, what can we achieve?' can lead to a clear description of potential outcomes, with insights into what you need to do in order to build both processes and commitment that will lead to these conclusions.

Mike recognised that when he was at his best, he could generate creative dialogue within a team and build strong motivation. He had received this positive affirmation in other teams he had led both inside and outside his work. Sometimes the energy to lead his team well was not there as day-to-day priorities got in the way. Mike knew he needed to be clear in his own mind how he would lead his senior team when he was at his best and then to articulate that approach to himself and to his two Deputy Heads.

To ensure that his leadership team delivered the agreed plan for the school, he needed to be giving clear overall steers and then be engaging with each member of the senior team about their priorities. When he was at his best, Mike was fully present and stimulating in discussion with his senior leaders. They felt valued and motivated. Mike recognised the approach he needed to bring and was determined to be at his best as often as he could, because he knew that his demeanour and approach would affect the leadership contribution of his entire senior team.

In practice

- Remember what others have told you about what you do when you are at your best

- Ask colleagues what they observe in you when you are at your best

- When you assess that your leadership has worked well, write down what you did that contributed to this outcome

- Allow the description of you at your best to evolve over time as your competences and confidence continue to grow

97 SHARE YOUR ASPIRATIONS FOR THE FUTURE

SHARING YOUR ASPIRATIONS for the team helps bind it together and builds a sense of common purpose and individual motivation.

The idea

Sharing aspirations for the future is not about describing an impossible dream. A good aspiration needs to be both doable and stretching. If as the team leader you set out an aspiration that colleagues do not think is realistic, they are likely to shrug their shoulders and be half-hearted in their approach. If the aspiration is within the bounds of the doable, there is more likely to be an engaged and enthusiastic response.

When a team has climbed a hill successfully, the leader can point to the next hill and with confidence assert that the summit of this second hill is also attainable. When an aspiration is within the realm of the doable, it can help create common purpose and a focusing of energy.

Sometimes an aspiration may seem doable to you but impossible to members of your team. Here it is important to share evidence about why you think it can be achieved, setting out rational arguments that the aspiration is doable. Your demeanour will communicate your emotional commitment to the shared enterprise.

There are times, however, when it may be unhelpful to share your aspirations for the future. You may be thinking longer-term, but the focus of your team members might, for the moment, be focused on the delivery of current plans. Talking too much too soon about your aspirations might be an unhelpful diversion.

Mike had an aspiration about a major capital project, rebuilding and improving the facilities for part of the school. Floating this idea too early could raise people's enthusiasm too quickly and divert them from delivering current objectives. He was careful to introduce some 'what if' comments in a low-key way, putting them in terms of a long-term future. He talked gently and thoughtfully about this long-term aspiration.

Others in the team mirrored this approach, which led to some good-quality conversations about what facilities would be useful in a new capital project and how a cost-effective case could be made for capital investment. Mike used questions that helped his team think through the possibilities without rushing to define unrealistic short-term goals.

In practice

- Give yourself time and space to explore aspirations for the future

- Believe it is helpful to have some aspirations for the future alongside what you are currently delivering

- Talk about your aspirations in a reflective and open-ended way, demonstrating you are listening to others

- Allow your aspirations for the future to be shaped in the light of the comments of people you trust

98 KNOW WHAT WILL NOURISH YOU AND UPHOLD YOU

KNOWING WHAT NOURISHES and upholds you is important in building the right type of equilibrium within you in order to handle future demands.

The idea

As you lead a team through demanding times, you need to be self-aware about what will renew your energy and what will sap it. It helps to be clear in your mind who you can talk to who will encourage you and help you develop your thinking going forward. You need people you can bounce ideas off and people who will stimulate your creativity and grow your curiosity.

Asking yourself the question, 'Which conversations nourish me and enthuse me?' can help identify who are the people it is good to spend time with because of the stimulus that their conversations provide.

It is right to ask who upholds you. Being frank about naming the people with whom there is a bond of trust and affection is important for your own personal stability. Your well-being depends on good, creative, energising conversations with some people, but it also depends on undemanding conversations with others who are committed to caring for you and upholding you. Ask yourself, 'Who gives me unconditional regard and love?'

What nourishes and upholds you might be spending time with the children in your life, or reading in areas outside work, or intense physical activity. Whatever nourishes you as you lead a team, commit time to doing it and talking about its effects on you.

What nourished Mike in being able to lead his senior team well was long-distance cycling, spending time with his family and being part of a small village church community. These three activities nourished him in different ways and complemented each other. He talked openly with members of his team about these three areas of life. Because of his openness, others were willing to talk about what nourished them. Mike talked about how he maintained his equilibrium at busy times, which set a thoughtful example for his colleagues.

In practice

- Recognise what nourishes you

- Give a high priority to activities that nourish you physically, emotionally, intellectually and spiritually

- Accept that allowing yourself to be nourished and upheld is necessary for your well-being

- Be explicit in your mind about which relationships uphold you and ensure you spend enough time nourishing these relationships

- Share with members of your team how you maintain your equilibrium and encourage them to be equally mindful about what nourishes and upholds them

99 · BE READY FOR UNEXPECTED OPPORTUNITIES

Success comes through a combination of focusing on current priorities and being open to unexpected opportunities.

The idea

Always be open to being surprised. When you are leading a team focused on a particular outcome, you will not want to be diverted. There is a path ahead which you want to stick to. The last thing you want is a distraction or an unexpected event that throws you off course. But you will want to be alert to what is happening outside your particular sphere. You need to be ready for the unexpected so that you can adapt your approach.

You are likely to be cautious about the unexpected as it could make your leadership task more difficult. But the unexpected is not always unhelpful. Your programme of work might have had to cope with scepticism from some, but that scepticism might be gradually waning, and previous critics might become potential allies. Others may see the merits of what your team is doing and want to build partnerships.

It is always worth looking out for opportunities and recognising that there are times when the impossible can become possible. Invite your team on a periodic basis to think about what might be the opportunities going forward. The context changes, different people are in key posts, financial considerations evolve.

Mike recognised that there was a danger of his team becoming complacent. Each secondary school tended to act in isolation and did not automatically look for partnership opportunities. The schools saw themselves in competition rather than valuing collaboration. Mike believed that for specialist subjects, collaboration between neighbouring schools could be a cost-effective way of using resources well. When the Head of a neighbouring school moved on, Mike saw this as a good opportunity to see what might be possible in terms of building partnership in specialist subject areas. What had previously been impossible now became a potential option if the new Head was open to this type of idea.

Mike wanted to build a good level of understanding with the new Head and sought to respond first to the new Head's agenda. Once the relationship had reached a constructive and trusting point, Mike began to float the idea of working in partnership in these specialist subject areas. Gradually they built a shared prospectus. What had looked impossible a year earlier now became an agreed plan going forward.

In practice

- Always be on the lookout for new opportunities

- Be ready to be surprised, and smile when you are surprised

- Have an open mind about opportunities you might like to take forward and be mindful about the right timing to suggest them

- Build trust and respect first before you seek to build an alliance to take forward a possible opportunity

- Adopt the belief that no matter how bleak a situation, there will always be constructive outcomes that flow from it

- See open-ended discussion about opportunities within a team as a valuable way of drawing on different strengths and perspectives

100 KEEP PASSING ON YOUR UNDERSTANDING AND YOUR LEARNING

IF YOU PASS ON your learning about leading a team well, you are encouraging and equipping the next generation, and reinforcing good practice in what you contribute.

The idea

Recently I met with the Principal of the college where I did a postgraduate degree in 1970. Jim Houston is now 93 and still passing on his understanding and learning. He continues to write and edit books and to mentor leaders in different spheres. Jim led teams at Oxford University and then in Vancouver, and continues to equip and stimulate the thinking of leaders of teams. The thoughtfulness and energy that Jim brings at 93 is an impressive example to many.

We are all building up greater knowledge and understanding about leading teams than we realise. We are instinctively developing our approach as we take account of what is working and not working, and are cognisant of the reactions of team members. We need good-quality feedback and self-assessment to recognise where we are becoming more effective in leading a team, and where we are developing bad habits that limit our effectiveness.

Passing on your understanding and your learning may sometimes be about tutoring others or setting out good practice. On other occasions, it might be about a coaching approach, where we encourage new team leaders to develop their own approaches. In these instances, we will be acting as a sounding board posing good questions rather than instructing.

Perhaps the most important learning to pass on is about an attitude of mind. Your encouragement to those developing their team leadership skills might be about bringing a more confident and open approach. You might be nurturing a focus on enabling and steering rather than doing and demanding. You will be bringing insights about how to set a constructive framework and clear expectations alongside creating a team environment that generates energy, innovation and partnership.

Mike saw some of the younger members of his leadership team as potential Deputy Heads and Heads. He spent time with each of these individuals, helping them to think through what type of leader they would be if they took on a more senior role and how they would lead their team effectively. He asked each of them to lead cross-cutting teams within the school to give them good-quality team leader experience.

Mike developed a coaching relationship with these individuals and was committed to their success. When one of them became Head Teacher of a neighbouring school, Mike was thrilled about the appointment and took immense satisfaction in the time he had invested in this person's development.

In practice

- Delight in passing on your understanding and learning as a team leader

- Recognise what type of contribution you can most effectively make with different individuals

- Use different parts of your repertoire in the way you develop prospective team leaders – sometimes tutoring them, sometimes sharing stories and on other occasions asking good questions

- Show your delight when members of your team move into bigger team leadership roles
- Ensure that those with potential gain wide experience of leading teams with different purposes and different types of members

BOOKS BY DR PETER SHAW

Mirroring Jesus as Leader. Cambridge: Grove, 2004.

Conversation Matters: How to engage effectively with one another. London: Continuum, 2005.

The Four Vs of Leadership: Vision, values, value-added, and vitality. Chichester: Capstone, 2006.

Finding Your Future: The second time around. London: Darton, Longman and Todd, 2006.

Business Coaching: Achieving practical results through effective engagement. Chichester: Capstone, 2007 (co-authored with Robin Linnecar).

Making Difficult Decisions: How to be decisive and get the business done. Chichester: Capstone, 2008.

Deciding Well: A Christian perspective on making decisions as a leader. Vancouver: Regent College Publishing, 2009.

Raise Your Game: How to succeed at work. Chichester: Capstone, 2009.

Effective Christian Leaders in the Global Workplace. Colorado Springs: Authentic/Paternoster, 2010.

Defining Moments: Navigating through business and organisational life. Basingstoke: Palgrave/Macmillan, 2010.

The Reflective Leader: Standing still to move forward. Norwich: Canterbury Press, 2011 (co-authored with Alan Smith).

Thriving In Your Work: How to be motivated and do well in challenging times. London: Marshall Cavendish, 2011.

Getting the Balance Right: Leading and managing well. Singapore: Marshall Cavendish, 2013.

Leading in Demanding Times. Cambridge: Grove, 2013 (co-authored with Graham Shaw).

The Emerging Leader: Stepping up in leadership. Norwich: Canterbury Press, 2013 (co-authored with Colin Shaw).

100 Great Personal Impact Ideas. Singapore: Marshall Cavendish, 2013.

100 Great Coaching Ideas. Singapore: Marshall Cavendish, 2014.

Celebrating Your Senses. Delhi: ISPCK, 2014.

Sustaining Leadership: Renewing your strength and sparkle. Norwich: Canterbury Press, 2014.

100 Great Team Effectiveness Ideas. Singapore: Marshall Cavendish, 2015.

FORTHCOMING BOOKS

Wake Up and Dream. Norwich: Canterbury Press, 2015.

ABOUT THE AUTHOR

DR PETER SHAW works with individuals, teams and groups to help them grow their strengths and tackle demanding issues confidently. His objective is to help individuals and teams clarify the vision of who they want to be, the values that are driving them, the value-added they want to bring and their sources of vitality.

His work on how leaders step up successfully into demanding leadership roles and sustain that success was recognised with the award of a Doctorate by Publication from the University of Chester in 2011.

Peter is a founding partner of Praesta Partners, an international specialist coaching business. His clients enjoy frank, challenging conversations leading to fresh thinking and new insights. It is the dynamic nature of the conversations that provides a stimulus for creating reflection and new action. He often works with Chief Executives and Board members taking on new roles and leading major organisational change. Peter has worked with a wide range of different leadership teams as they tackle new challenges.

Peter has worked with Chief Executives and senior teams in a range of different sectors and countries. He has led workshops on such themes as 'Riding the Rapids', 'Seizing the Future', 'Thriving in your Work', 'Being an Agile Leader' and 'Building Resilience' across five continents.

Peter has held a wide range of Board posts covering finance, personnel, policy, communications and delivery. He worked in five UK Government departments (Treasury, Education, Employment, Environment and Transport). He delivered major national changes such as radically different pay arrangements for teachers, a huge expansion in nursery education and employment initiatives which helped bring unemployment below a million.

He led the work on the merger of the UK Government Departments of Education and Employment. As Finance Director General he managed a £40bn budget and introduced radical changes in funding and accountability arrangements. In three Director General posts he led strategic development and implementation in major policy areas. In 2000 he was awarded a CB by the Queen for his contribution to public service.

Peter has written a sequence of influential leadership books. He is a Visiting Professor of Leadership Development at Newcastle University Business School and a Visiting Professor in the Business, Enterprise and Lifelong Learning Department at the University of Chester. He has worked with senior staff at Brighton University and with postgraduate students at Warwick University Business School and at Regent College in Vancouver. He is an Honorary Professorial Fellow at St John's College, Durham University. He was awarded an Honorary Doctorate (Doctor of Civil Law) by Durham University in 2015 for 'outstanding service to public life and the the Council of St John's College'.

Peter is a Reader (licensed lay minister) in the Anglican Church and has worked with senior church leaders in the UK, North America and Asia. His inspiration comes from long-distance walks: he has completed seventeen long-distance walks in the UK, including the St Cuthbert's Way, the South Downs Way, the Yorkshire Wolds Way, the Yorkshire Dales Way, the Ribble Way, the Speyside Way, the St Oswald's Way and the Great Glen Way. Peter and his wife, Frances, have three grown-up children who are all married, and a growing number of grandchildren.